Do The Write Thing

7 Steps To Publishing Success

Do The Write Thing

7 Steps To Publishing Success

by
Kwame
Alexander with Nina Foxx

MW Books
A Limited Liability Corporation
Austin, Texas

Quote in Introduction-Al Haji Sy, Sene-Gambian National Poet

First printing 2002

Published by Manisy Willows Books,LLC
701 Capitol of Texas Highway
Box 1202 Building C
Austin, Texas 78746
www.manisywillows.com

This book contains information gathered from several sources. Neither the authors nor the publishers engaged in rendering any legal, psychological or accounting advice. The authors and publisher disclaim any personal liability, either directly or indirectly, for advice or information presented. They assume no responsibility for errors, inaccuracies, omissions, or any inconsistency herein. Any slights of people, places, publishers, books or organizations are unintentional.

ISBN:0-9678959-6-0
Library of Congress: 2001 129132

Cover and Book Design by Kim Greyer Graphic Design
Editor: Barbara Lewis Washington, Ph.D.

Associate Publisher: Brandie Scott

10 9 8 7 6 5 4 3 2 1

Acknowledgments

A book such as this is the result of a long, and sometimes arduous education. To try and thank the many people who contributed to my knowledge store would mean listing hundreds, if not more, of names. I will try, as I believe giving recognition is a pre-requisite to receiving rewards.

I am grateful first and foremost to my father, Dr. E Curtis Alexander, who taught me everything I ever needed (and wanted) to know about book publishing. Two mentors who have eagerly imparted their publishing wisdom over the years: Haki R. Madhubuti, Founder of Third World Press, and Ralph Eubanks, Director of Publishing, Library of Congress. The writers and industry professionals who read this manuscript in its infancy and offered invaluable advice: Tracy Grant, Lori Bryant-Woolridge, Tony Lindsay, Pamela Brown, Mike Williams and Stephanie Stanley Alexander, Jennifer Rhodes. My agent, Audra Barrett, who is young, talented and on her way to The Country (Thanks for what's to come).

I am equally thankful to those individuals who were directly, or indirectly helpful in the preparation of this manuscript. Barbara Alexander, Irwin and Sheila Alexis, Shia Barnett, Manie Baron, Sylvia Dianne Beverly-Patterson, Stephenie Brooks, Guichard Cadet, Antwan Clinton, Judy Cooper, William Cox, Judith Curtis, Stacey Evans, Sydnye Oyugi, Mike Williams, Marvin Hamilton, Monica Harris, Scott D. Haskins, Troy Johnson, Joseph K. Jones, Mondella Jones, Michon Lartique, Sherri Lee, Tonya Matthews, Nichole D. Shields, Crystal Stanley, Angela Turnbull, Laura Whitener, Van Whitfield, Gregg Wilhelm and Carol Williams.

Special Thanks to my editor, Dr. Barbara Lewis, my co-writer, Nina Foxx, and my Publisher, Beryl Horton, who helped make this multi-year project, a pleasant reality.

Lastly, the patience of my daughter Nandi, and my wife Samaraca, is only matched by their beauty and support of my literary pursuits.

For

Nandi
Ndali
Sydney
Jay
Mykel

and their unborn musicals, ballets, paintings and BOOKS . . .
age quod agis

Additional Books

Also by Kwame Alexander

Just Us : Poems and Counterpoems 1986-1995
Tough Love
360 Anthology
Kupenda: Love Poems
360° Poetry Anthology

Also by Nina Foxx

Dippin' My Spoon

Contact

How to Contact the Authors

blackwordsinc@cs.com
or
manisywillowsbooks@austin.rr.com
512/347-9995

Table of Contents

Preface

I've always wondered about the difference between the preface and foreword of a book. Where does the introduction fit? What about the prologue? This line of questioning could go on and on. According to **Webster's Dictionary***, the preface is the "preliminary statement in a book by an author or editor, setting forth the book's purpose." Well, that's simple enough.*

Do The Write Thing (DTWT) is like Publishing 101. It is designed for the novice who wants to learn the ABC's of book publishing. This reading will be similar to the first time you rode a bike. Remember when your father guided you down the sidewalk day after day? Then one Saturday he let you ride by yourself. Just like that. And while you did fall a few times, eventually, through practice, courage and ingenuity, you mastered it. One day you even "popped a wheelie." DTWT is pithy (like this preface). Unlike most publishing how-to books, which seem to get mired down in every possible detail and tedious direction, my publisher and I decided that DTWT would give you a general map drawn in bright colors, and leave it up to you to chart your own course. I will impart my knowledge if you promise to tap into your creativity. My purpose is to teach you the mechanics of book publishing so that you feel confident enough to "ride by yourself." Ready?

Prefatory Note

This book is intended primarily as a working tool for writers looking to self-publish. Of course, others will find these instructions inform-ative, insightful and, I hope, invaluable. While the information provided here is comprehensive, by no means do I exhaust the plethora of detail of which publishing consists. My humble recommendation is that you read through the entire book once, and then return to it, step-by-step, when you are ready to publish.

Introduction

Foolish is the man who possesses a valuable book and loans it out.
But more foolish is the man who borrows a valuable book
and returns it.
-Al Haji Sy, Sene-Gambian National Poet

Today is Christmas. I am in Louisiana visiting my wife's family. It is the first time I have been away from my immediate family during the Christmas holiday season. I have learned that sometimes life requires you to move outside of your comfort zone, in order to experience newness, growth, change (and real Gumbo), or as Spencer Johnson would say "Follow Your Cheese."

Having written three poetry books, and edited one collection of cultural criticism, penning a creative non-fiction how-to book was a daunting task. This book found its way in the bottom desk drawer several times over the past four years. Writing poetry has always been exciting, therapeutic, and downright fun for me. Writing a how-to book couldn't be any of those things, as there were rules that had to be followed. Boring rules. Like being away from family, I was unfamiliar with this literary territory. That frightened me. So I did what every intelligent poet does when learning how to do something besides writing poetry. *I read*. There are secrets, plans, ideas and plenty of magic inside of books. I read every how-to-publish book *twice*. I read everything I could about writing non-fiction. I read creative non-fiction (David Sedaris really cracks me up). I even read fiction (J. California Cooper is so conversational, makes you think she's in your living room). Finally, I knew the manner/style in which I wanted to talk to you, the reader. I now had the confidence to ride by myself; however, one obstacle remained. As there were hundreds of books on publishing, what would make you choose *my* book in this competitive marketplace? Furthermore, why did I even decide to write this particular book, considering the many choices budding writers and publishers already have?

When I started publishing six years ago, I was fortunate enough to publish a best-selling novel written by a new writer from Washington, DC. As a result, the word soon got around that I was giving opportunities to young writers. At first, this was a good thing. It provided me with a wealth of material from which to choose, and it gave hope to the budding writers. Soon, the manuscripts started pouring in, over twenty a week to be exact. I was overwhelmed, being a small press with only one person on staff (including me). There was no way possible I could read each of the submissions, let alone publish even a few. Disgruntled writers were calling and sending letters asking why they hadn't heard from me in months (some may have shown up at my door, but I was smart enough to only list a PO Box in all literature). Surely, there was a solution to this madness. A friend of mine suggested that I conduct a seminar, teaching writers how to self-publish. While I'd never organized or promoted a seminar, I did study theatre in college, and I did know publishing.

In 1996, I facilitated my first publishing seminar. It was called *Do The Write Thing: How To Publish your Book in Ten Easy Steps*. For weeks, I gathered information, forms, statistics, applications, books, magazines, and numerous eferences. I figured that dividing the book publishing process into ten steps would keep my *talk* manageable, and it well within my promotional plans (any writer, anywhere, any book-no problem!) My notes would have pleased any professor. Notebooks were filled. As my Aunt Gracie would say, "I was together." Upon arriving at a local university classroom, which I booked for pennies, I discovered that I'd eft my notes. The NOTES! What happened for the next four hours (it was a half-day seminar for $25) was a combination of improvisation, creative storytelling, and childhood remembrances. Somehow I found time to share The Seven Steps. You may ask what happened to the "Ten" steps. Well, since I'd left my notes, I was relying on my memory, which only held seven of them (I still can't remember what the other three are). In all, I had a great time relaying my experiences with specific books, and more importantly the sixty participants left with the write/right tools to successfully self-publish. It was a great balance of knowledge, example, repetition (remember, I had no notes), and humor. And t worked.

Over the past five years, I've produced nearly one hundred of these DTWT seminars for writers, publishers, teachers, and other professionals. Several of these participants have gone on to publish their works, some even twice. When illing out the post-seminar survey, the most common comment is: "The way you do the seminar is so informational yet entertaining, it really makes the steps memorable. I didn't know publishing was so much fun." Of course, I expect this, since I've done every single seminar just like the first one: no notes, creative storytelling, the seven steps, and every now and then when I feel the magic, I'll share a poem.

Publishing is a wonderful industry in which to work. This book is about the process of taking your book idea from concept to printed product. It is based on my one hundred publishing seminars. The seminar was my way of teaching writers the basic fundamentals and tools of self-publishing, while protecting my hide (Since I couldn't publish everybody, at least I could teach everybody how to publish themselves). The good thing is the tools in this book are fairly simple to use, sort of like a hammer or screwdriver. The flip side is these tools don't function alone. You will need to use a little elbow grease and get those creative juices flowing. The process of writing, editing, rewriting, designing, printing, marketing and distributing your literary masterpiece is tedious, but taking control of your literary destiny is electrifying. In addition to these steps, I've added a section on publishing and promoting poetry, and at the end of each chapter there are worksheets for your convenience and a list of additional practical resources.

Today, my wife and I passed out Christmas gifts: *James Earl Jones Reads The Bible*, *The Giver*, *Bill Cosby's Little Bill Series*, *If Men Are Like Buses Then How Do I Catch One?* (for my gregarious sister-in-law), and a host of other feel good tomes. I was overcome by the valuable possibilities books offer to the human soul. The best reason for writing this book is to give you the opportunity to share with us your secrets, plans, ideas and magic. Don't worry; I won't keep you long. It's only seven steps. And if you're really inspired, maybe you'll even "pop a wheelie".

— K. A.
December 25, 2000

Step 1.

Conjuring the Muse:
Writing Your Book

Step 1. Conjuring the Muse:
Writing Your Book

I t's been said that almost anyone can write a book. What this chapter aims to do is help you polish and publish a good one. If you are indeed preparing to publish a quality product, the first step is to focus on conceptualizing and writing the best book possible. For this reason, I have chosen to begin this book with a discussion on writing. Have you decided what your book will be about? What type of preparation, research and development is necessary, if any? What is your motivation for writing the book? How does that affect what you're writing and why? Are you writing to publish for a mass audience, a niche-market, or specific group (e.g. church, family, etc.)? All these decisions and more will help you solidify your ideas into a finished manuscript.

The "Why?" Question

Do you know why you want to write your book? I remember working with a retired-teacher-turned-writer who wanted to publish a history of her family. She told me that there were to be over five hundred of her relatives from twenty-five states at the family reunion. It was her dream to publish a collection of family photos, remembrances, recipes, legends and biographies and sell one copy to every member of her family. With such a large and dispersed family, she felt it was important to preserve their legacy and history for present and future generations, no matter where they resided. This writer clearly knew her motivation from the start: to preserve her family's legacy. Of course, this motivation provided a solid foundation for her writing and eventual publishing.

Do you know your answer to the "Why" question? You may feel compelled to document your local history. You may want to share your poetic expressions of love with others, and help make the world a better place. Writing for some is strictly motivated by a yearning to WRITE. Some just have it in their blood, so to speak. Then there are writers who go to school, study literature, and spend day and night creating the next great American novel.

The "Why" question will help you determine what your subject matter is, what type of book you will write, and who your audience is. For instance, if your primary goal is to make lots of money, you may decide to write the type of book that the industry recognizes as a "hot-seller." Recognize your purpose, as it will dictate your agenda. Every book, like a business meeting, starts with an agenda. The worksheet that follows this chapter can help you visualize your end goal: to be a published author.

I met him at a book signing for one of my authors. Let's just say his name was ***That Guy***. He was interested in self-publishing his romance novel. I was surprised, as you don't find a whole lot of men writing "love fiction." He'd written the novel as an act of therapy after a painful relationship (what a way to deal with your baggage). After finishing it, he decided that it was pretty good, publishable even. Anyway, he showed me his properly-formatted manuscript, and some promotional materials that he'd produced (T-shirts, bookmarks, pens, CD's, baseball caps, posters, flyers, and plenty more). All this hype about a book that had not even been published yet. He obviously understood the power of marketing. But did he know books?

I asked him why he wanted to self-publish, and he answered that he initially wanted to get a book deal from a major publisher but no one thought it would sell. Thus, he decided to do it himself, show them it would make money, and wait for them to call him with "offers on the table." Eventually, he would be able to quit his job. ***That Guy*** was very focused; he knew his motivation intimately, and it propelled him forward. The only concern I had was that he wanted to release the book in two months. I was young and the challenge was exciting. I decided to help him.

The "What?" Factor

Considerable thought should to be given to picking a subject, and there are plenty of places to look. In each edition of your local newspaper there are hundreds of ideas for the next great book. Likewise, many writers find that the lives of their own family members are matter for interesting drama. Consider your talents and the amount of time you can devote to your book. Recognize your motivation. Examine your own personal interests, professional experience, or some experience or incident that has inspired your creativity juices. Often times, an interesting idea will pop into your head while sitting at a red light, or on a slow day at the office. For those of you who don't have this luxury, however, brainstorming is always a good idea. Search the Internet for interesting news and information. Write down book concepts that you would enjoy reading. Visit your local library or bookstore and look around. We will call this process *Conjuring the Muse*.

Some authors prefer to choose a title before starting the book, as it serves as a guiding light. Still, others choose a title much later, once they are in the writing process or have completed it. The choice is yours. Pick something that represents your subject, its theme, and your purpose. As a budding writer, there are worlds of ideas for your discovery. Consider those that are in line with your purpose. It'll make your job a lot easier.

Genre, pronounced "John-ruh," is the specific category of literature, marked by a distinctive style, form, or content. The genre you select is simply a matter of choice and writing skill. Let's take a look at some genres and the authors who fit in each category:

1. Commercial Fiction (Billie Letts, E. Lynn Harris, Nicholas Sparks, etc.)
2. Literary Fiction (Toni Morrison, Ha Jin, Charles Frazier, etc.)
3. Creative Non-Fiction (Michael Eric Dyson, Spalding Gray, Veronica Chambers, etc.)
4. Poetry (Michael Collier, Sonia Sanchez, Jewel, etc.)
5. Children's Literature (E. B. Lewis, Eric Carle, Adjoa Burrows, etc.)
6. Autobiography/Memoir (Frank McCourt, asha bandele, James McBride, etc.)
7. Humor (Dave Barry, Kim Coles, Bill Cosby, etc.)
8. Self-Help/Medical/Inspirational (Andrew Weil, Iyanla Vanzant, Stephen Covey, etc.)
9. Business/Money (Andrew Posner, Spencer Johnson, Suze Orman, etc.)
10. Mystery/Crime (Nelson Demille, Patricia Cornwell, Tony Lindsay, etc.)
11. Romance (Candace Poarch, Danielle Steele, Sandra Kitt, etc.)

There are many more types of writing to explore and discover. Feel free to cross boundaries and incorporate elements of more than one genre.

Writing is a creative process, thus your own creativity must be tapped immensely. As mentioned earlier, this first step is key, and fueling your imagination is extremely important in establishing your literary direction. Be relentless taking these first steps in the publishing process, as you have nothing to lose (except your privacy after your book sells a million copies and you become an instant celebrity). Lastly, once you open the floodgates, the ideas will start flowing, and your muse will be ready to work. So, nurture and enjoy.

The "How?" Plan

Now, that you have decided upon your motivation for writing and publishing, the next big decision is how best to develop your concept. Remember that the more preparation you can do before writing, the more time you will save in the end. Research your ideas so that you can write accurately and with confidence.

I once listened to a writer speak at a literary conference about an exciting idea he had for an essay. He wanted to compare the lyrics and style of a contemporary rapper with a blues singer fifty years his senior. While the writer was very knowledgeable about popular culture and rap music, he was not too aware of the history of the blues. He immersed himself in the study of the sociology, economics and origin of the Blues in America. From reading texts, to listening to the legends, he was able to develop a greater understanding of blues music, which then allowed him to better relate to the two forms of music, and inevitably the two musicians.

Whether you are writing historical or romance fiction, how-to or cooking, knowing as much information about your topic is a writer's responsibility and will make your work richer and more credible. Just as there is good cooking and bad cooking (can you imagine someone messing up pancakes?), there is good writing and bad writing. Once you have decided what type of writing you are doing, it is imperative to learn the rules of that particular genre. Maybe you majored in English or received an MFA in creative writing; perhaps you've attended poetry workshops, or you may just be a natural. Whatever your case, the process of learning to write should not be taken for granted.

The writing workshop is the most common approach to honing your writing craft. In a typical workshop, writers read samples of their work to other writers, who then critique and offer editorial suggestions for the work. This is like learning by trial and error (remember the bicycle?). Check your local community college and community centers, as published writers often teach very inexpensive one-day and ongoing classes in various genres. Of course, we all know that the best-kept secrets are found in your local library. Here's the best way I've learned to enhance my writing skills: reading books about writing and reading books in specific genres. Reading anything and everything will help you develop your style. It is an established fact that all writers steal, *oops*, borrow from other writers. Nothing is new under the sun. Former President Clinton's favorite mystery writer, Walter Mosley, is a literary amalgamation of Langston Hughes and Raymond Chandler. Of course, he has his own style and flavor, but we can see its origins. (Warning: This is not the same thing as copying a writer's voice, as in the hundreds of non-creative Terry McMillan knock-off's that surfaced in the 90's.) Learning how to write well comes with time and study. The basics of grammar, punctuation, and English composition are must-know skills for the developing writer. Barbara, a teacher and writer friend of mine often tells her high school students "Know the rules before you break them."

The Final Stage

Once I attended a theatre master class taught by some of the giants of theatre from the 1960's and 70's: Douglass Turner Ward, Woodie King, and the brilliant and beautiful Cicely Tyson. Afterwards, I went up to Mr. Ward and proudly proclaimed that I was a playwright, at which point he pointedly questioned, "Well, what have you finished?" What a strange question, I thought, especially since I had over seventy-five pages of four different plays. But I hadn't finished one of them. This was the first valuable lesson I learned about being a writer. First and foremost, complete something. This is where your daily schedule comes in handy. I suggest writing every day, perhaps one hour or two hours, or if you are really serious, five or six. We've all heard of the famous writer who wrote her first book every morning from 4 am to 6:30 am, before work, and then rewrote every night after dinner from 7:00 pm to 10:00 pm. While writing this book, I was determined to write a minimum number of pages per day. Decide when you like to write best and come up with a daily or weekly schedule. You may find yourself straying from time to time, but since you have the schedule, you will always be able to get back on the right path. Believe it or not, most writers find this process of staying focused on writing to be the most challenging. How long the writing process takes will depend on your focus and plan of action. Whether it will take two weeks or two years is entirely up to you. In the end, discipline will separate the authors from the wannabe authors.

We've approached the end of this journey. It's time to find a comfortable place in your home, the local library (or if you've got some money to spend, a suite at Le Mondrian in Los Angeles) where you can complete an outline for your book and start writing. I could write an entire book on writing (There are plenty out there), but the bike is really on your street now. Just ride. You've conjured your muse, now it's time to write your book, one word, one day at a time. Bring together all the tools we've discussed and put your pen to paper. First, second, third . . . final draft, here we come. But first, let's review, and see if you can answer a few questions about your book.

Worksheet 1:
Conjuring the Muse

1. Decide what you want to write about. Write three topics that interest you.

   a) _____

   b) _____

   c) _____

2. Develop your Concept. Write a three-line summary of it here.

   _____

   _____

   _____

3. Who is your target audience? Adults? Children? A specific geographical region? Write that here.

   _____

   _____

4. Decide what genre your work will fall into. Write that here.

   _____

   _____

5. Figure out when and where you are going to write. Make a commitment to yourself. Now write that.
   (e.g.: I am going to write for three hours every day in the privacy of my office.)

   _____

   My Commitment to Myself:

   _____

   _____

   _____

Selected Reading

Bogen, Nancy. *How To Write Poetry.* New York: McMillan, 1994.

Cameron, Julia. *The Artist's Way: A Spiritual Craft to Higher Creativity.* New York: G. P. Putnam Sons, 1995.

Field, Marion. *The Writer's Guide to Research: An Invaluable Guide to Gathering Materials for Articles, Novels and Non-fiction.* Trans-Atlantic Publications, 2000.

Frey, James. *How to Write a Damn Good Novel.* New York: St. Martin's Press, 1987.

Goldberg, Natalie. *Writing Down the Bones.* Shambhala Publications, 1998.

Holm, Kirsten (editor). *Writer's Market 2001.* Writer's Digest Books, 2000.

Kgositsile, Keorapetse. *Approaches to Poetry Writing.* Chicago: Third World Press, 1994.

*King, Stephen. *On Writing: A Memoir of Craft.* New York: Pocket Books, 2001.

*Miller, E. Ethelbert. *The Making of an African American Writer.* New York: St. Martin's Press, 2000.

Poynter, Dan. *Writing Nonfiction: Turning Thoughts into Books.* California: Para Publishing, 1999.

Memoirs on writing; these proved invaluable to my continued understanding of the craft.

Step 2.

Fine-Tuning
Your Manuscript

Step 2. Fine-Tuning Your Manuscript

When the manuscript is finally turned over to an editor, we expect sound advice. Instead, we end up with pages and pages of our words painted over with what appears to be marks from a red-penned maniac, disguised as an editor. That's what editors do. If you are to publish the best quality book possible, it is imperative that you first hire someone who knows how to make your book better, and second, you must trust that person.

Who They Are & What They Do

Editors are trained to make your manuscript better, in terms of style, substance, consistency and grammar. Editing is the process by which your manuscript is corrected, modified

and made acceptable to your reading public by a professional editor.

My sister had a pink ten-speed and I had a silver beach
cruiser. They both had wheels, but each functioned a little
differently. Such is the case with editors. Let's briefly look at a
few types of editors who exist within (or as an adjunct to)
your publishing company. Keep in mind, there is overlap, as
some editors perform several functions.

- *Acquisition Editors* are in charge of reviewing and rating
  incoming manuscripts for possible publication. They
  typically supervise the publication process. If you choose
  to publish other writers in addition to yourself, you will
  become one of these.

- *Content* or *Line Editors* are known simply as 'Editors' and
  they are responsible for cutting, rearranging, and adding
  content to improve a book's style and story. This is the
  person with whom you will develop the infamous
  love/hate relationship. Keep in mind that the editor
  usually LOVES BOOKS, and you are paying for this
  service. In the same way that doctors are custodians of
  our physical well being, editors "heal" our words. So
  listen to what s/he says! (Most of the time!)

- *Developmental Editors* serve the same purpose as Content
  Editors, but they tend to focus on non-fiction, history and
  works that are more research-based. In addition to being
  an editor, the developmental editor is usually a scholar in
  a particular field of study.

- *Copyeditors* are the red-penned maniacs that we referred
  to earlier. It is their job to find all the grammatical,
  spelling and punctuation errors in your book. I cannot
  stress how important they are. *Maybe I can:* It's one thing

to find 75 typographical errors (typos) in your book; it's another thing to find them *after* the book has been published.

- *Proofreaders* are basically the same as copyeditors. Often times a proofreader will be the last person to see a book before it goes *on press* (to the printer). Proofreaders will generally check for typos and formatting irregularities that missed the copyeditor's eyes. Also, sometimes this person will perform a comparison proof, which determines if all the errors that the copyeditor caught were indeed fixed.

Earlier, I mentioned how **That Guy** wanted to publish his novel in two months. To make that happen he gave up some things, including the copyediting phase. He thought the editor caught most of the grammatical errors, punctuation and typos. He wanted to eventually sell the book to Doubleday or Random House (or some other Major Publisher), yet he didn't see the importance of proofing his book to present the best-possible product. Contrary to my suggestions, he decided to forego a copyedit. The ramifications of this decision came a little later, and I hated being right.

For the most part, you will be using a content editor and some combination of a copyeditor/proofreader. Of course, you will need a "clean eyes" person. The "clean eyes" person is usually the one friend you have who notices even the smallest typo in the ingredients section on the Campbell's Chicken Noodle soup can. This is the friend you love to hate.

It's important to hire only the most qualified professionals for your editing work. Ideally, you want to hire an editor who does this for a living. If you are writing a business book, you want to work with an editor who has sensibilities and knowledge in the particular industry. If you are writing a cookbook, you want to work with an editor who specializes in cooking. Whatever your genre, find a corresponding editor. There are some editors who can edit fiction, poetry, romance, and business, etc., but most specialize. You can talk to other writers to get their recommendations. Most professional editors charge either an hourly rate ($45-$125 per hour), or a per page fee ($5-$20 per page). Earlier in the book, we talked about using your creativity. Consider this: English professors and teachers often double as editorial consultants and editors, as do writers. When you think about it, what better person to edit your manuscript than a Creative Writing or English teacher, who spends day after day teaching the art of good writing to teenagers and twenty-something's? Perhaps you have a friend who is a teacher or graduate student and can serve as your editor. You might also find that low-cost or free editor through your local writer's league. Make sure the person you hire is a professional. Your writing must meet the highest editorial standard if you are to be considered a credible writer and publisher.

In addition to checking for clarity, grammatical errors

and typos, your editor must deliver in a timely manner. I remember consulting with a first-time novelist who had a friend who was a newspaper journalist by day, and a struggling novelist by night. I determined that the friend was qualified, and she was brought on board as the editor. After negotiating a flat fee of $500 (considerably less than we would have had to pay a professional editor), she began the process of editing the novel. While we were pleased with her work (a "professional" could not have done a better line edit), we did miss a few deadlines. It's a give and take situation when you are dealing with "by night" editors. Fortunately, we built in enough extra time, so the negative impact was minimal.

You Have an Editor, Now What?

It's time to give your content editor a hard copy (print out) of your manuscript. You probably don't want to give the editor a digital file, as you may not want to accept all suggested edits, and a paper copy is easier to manipulate visually. The duration of time that the manuscript is in the editor's hands depends on variables such as page length, genre, complexity, and more. One of my previous poetry books took all of two weeks to edit, as compared with this book, which took two months. Still, some projects can take even a year to complete a thorough edit.

This is a good place to mention that for some of the steps in this book, it will be necessary for you to perform several tasks at one time. For instance, while the editor has your book, it may be a good idea for you to focus your business energies on building your publishing company. After all, whether you plan to publish other writers, or just your one book, you will have expenses and revenue (significant revenue, we hope). Thus, you will need to start a fully functional publishing business. I will discuss this further in Step 3.

Once the book is back from the editor, the *real writing* begins. This is the stage where you've finally established a bike-riding rhythm (and you feel pretty good about it). Now you are faced with friends who have reflectors on their spokes, horns on their handlebars, and speedometers. You've never paid attention to the extra things, as you were just trying to learn how to ride. It's time to add more function-ality to your manuscript. The instructions are written on each page (every other, if you're lucky) of your book. The editor has given you comments and suggested changes to make your book better. A literary novelist I worked with a few years back had written a touching and spiritual coming-of-age story about five generations of women in the same family. The story was compelling, but the editor commented that she could never fully enjoy the plot because she could not keep up with the many integral characters that lived in the pages. It became too confusing to figure out who was being talked about in a given paragraph. The editor's suggestion to add a family tree after the prologue solved this issue (and added an extra two pages to the length of the book, which took us over the 200 mark). Revise your manuscript based on the editing suggestions (nee, *demands*) of the editor. Many writers consider this phase of the process to be the *real writing* that takes place. In a sense it's true: writing *is* rewriting!

It's usually a good idea to send the book back to the editor at least once. The amount of times the manuscript passes back and forth between you and the editor will vary. You can make that determination. Our discussion about copyediting and proofreading will continue in Step 4.

There are traditionally three sections to a book. The main text or body, we've just discussed. The first is the front matter, the series of pages that appear before the body. In sequential order, the pages are: the half-title page, which has only the title of the book; a blank page; the recto-title page, which expands the half-title by adding a subtitle, author's name, and the publisher; the verso or copyright page which lists the permissions, copyrights, ISBN and Library of Congress numbers, designer credits, printing history, publisher information, and possibly more; the dedication page; and another blank page. The remaining pages of the front matter will vary depending on your needs: table of contents, acknowledgments, preface, foreword, and introduction.

The final section of the book is the back matter. This section is found after the body, and may include the index, endnotes, glossary, reference list, the author's biography, and perhaps an excerpt from your next book. Once again, you should look at other similar books, to determine the elements of your back matter.

It's not quite time to celebrate, but you're halfway there. Making it this far in the publishing process means you're still riding.

Completing Step 2 should give you a sense of relief. The literary grunt work is now done, and we have fine-tuned your manuscript. As we get closer to our destination, a strong balance of the creative and the business will be necessary for success. Hang on!

Worksheet 2:
Fine-Tuning Your Masterpiece

1. Perform a spell-check on your manuscript and print it out. There are some errors that just cannot be seen on the computer screen. Also, make sure you've incorporated all the book's components.

   _____

   _____

   _____

2. Re-read. Spell check alone is not enough. For instance, if you mean stationery and actually write stationary, spell check will never catch it. Read your work as if you did not write it, make corrections, and re-write.

   _____

   _____

   _____

3. Print out a clean copy of your manuscript. _(One technique I like to use is to give the manuscript to ten critical friends/associates who will tell the absolute truth and won't mind hurting my feelings.)_ Re-write again based on their feedback. Now you're ready for your editors.

   _____

   _____

   _____

4. List the sources of some potential editors. List specific names if you know them. Write down the sources, then call them and get bids for their rates. Be sure to find out how long the editors will take with your manuscript.

   _____

   _____

   _____

Selected Reading

Einsohn, Amy. *The Copyeditor's Handbook: A Guide for Book Publishing and Corporate Communications: With Exercises and Answer Keys.* California: University of California Press, 2000.

Grossman, John. *The Chicago Manual of Style: The Essential Guide for Writers, Editors, and Publishers (14th Edition).* Chicago: University of Chicago Press, 1994.

Kinzie, Mary: *A Poet's Guide to Poetry (Chicago Guides to Writing, Editing and Publishing).* Chicago: University of Chicago Press, 1999.

Ross-Larson, Bruce. *Edit Yourself: A Manual for Everyone Who Works With Words.* New York: W. W. Norton & Company, 1996.

Smith, Debra A. *Powerful Proofreading Skills: Tips, Techniques and Tactics (Fifty-Minute Series).* Crisp Publications, 1995.

Sullivan, K. D. *Go Ahead, Proof It!.* Barrons, 1996.

Venolia, Jan and Ellen Sasaki (Illustrator). *Rewrite Right!: Your Guide to Perfectly Polished Prose: 2nd Edition.* Ten Speed Press, 2000.

Step 3.

Building a Business:
Starting a Publishing Company

Step 3. Building a Business:
Starting a Publishing Company

Starting a Publishing Company

Laying the groundwork for a new publishing company may not seem like loads of fun, but if you are still serious about being successful (and getting on Oprah), it's required work. I intentionally made this the third step, so you would have ample time to be a "writer." With that behind you (for now), it is time to *become* Bill Gates. The other side of your brain, the more practical side, will be necessary for this chapter. I knew a self-published writer who, during his book parties, would put on a snazzy vest when he read from the work, and take it off when it was time for the attendees to purchase copies. He needed to present himself as an artist and a businessman. In order to make money and be successful as a publisher, and as a business person, you must think dollars and sense. Learning how to operate a business is only the beginning. A major portion of Step 3 is learning about the world of publishing and how you fit into the big scheme of things. If you want to be considered a credible player, your attention to industry and entrepreneurial detail is as important as the dotted i's and crossed t's in your manuscript.

Operating a Business

Being a first-time entrepreneur is a lot like diving into a 10-foot pool without knowing how to swim. The focus here is not to present detailed information on running a business, but instead to only mention the immediate administrative and operational tasks set before you. Now, this information may not seem like loads of fun, but an understanding of the basics of business administration is crucial to success in your venture.

- Choose a name that represents the image you want your publishing company to exhibit today and in the future. Some companies choose names that start with the letter A, as they will always be first in many listings, including Yellow Pages and some Internet Searches. Many publishers were named after their founders, and are now household names: Alfred Knopf, Simon & Schuster, Henry Holt, William Morrow, and Harper-Collins.
- Like the name, your company logo will be the brand that your future customers come to recognize. A brand can be a powerful tool used to sell other books published by your company. A local artist or graphic designer can

assist you with creating one. Your logo will appear on the spine of your books, on the copyright page, as well as on all marketing and print materials.

- Decide on a location for your business. Many small and self-publishers operate out of their homes, often using a den or the basement as headquarters. While this reduces your financial overhead, it can sometimes become burdensome, especially when you want a break from work. It's a good idea to maintain a designated workspace, some place that you can "leave" once you're ready to "go home." In most cities, there are business incubators where small businesses are provided with office space and other resources, literally for pennies. If you are looking to rent business property, observe real estate in areas where you'd like to be, and inquire with an agent.

- Secure a business phone & fax line, business checking account (don't forget the check card!), and a PO Box to serve as your mailing address. You probably don't want unexpected writers coming to your home office to pitch their latest project.

- Your stationery is comprised of your business cards, letterhead, and your envelopes, with logo and name, for correspondence. Along with your logo, these components make up corporate identity. Either hire a graphic designer to assist you, or, with the basic desktop publishing program, you can do this yourself.

- Purchase software and computer hardware equipped with enough memory for word processing (e.g. Microsoft Word™, Word Perfect™), record-keeping (Quickbooks Pro™, Peachtree Accounting™) and the Internet (e.g. AOL,

Mindspring™). If you intend to pursue publishing long-term, it would be wise to invest in enough memory for the desktop publishing or typesetting (e.g. Quark Xpress™, Pagemaker™), and graphic design software (e.g. Corel Draw™, Adobe Illustrator™ and Photoshop™).

- The type of legal form that you select for your new business can be crucial in determining your success. There are four legal forms to choose from: sole proprietorship, partnership, corporation, and limited liability corporation. No one form is better than another. Each has its advantages and disadvantages. The important thing is to determine the legal forms that will work best for you. There are several books listed at the end of this chapter that will help you make sure you have selected a legal form that is appropriate for your business. You can always start at one and move to another when the time is appropriate.

- There are local, state and federal regulations that must be adhered to in order to protect you. Locally, consult your clerk's office for information on business licenses, taxes, permits, zoning regulations and fictitious business name statements. Your state department can let you know if you need a seller's permit. The federal government requires you to have an employer identification number (EIN). In some cases, this EIN may be your social security number. The US Patent Office can handle your requests for registered trademarks and patents.

- A good business plan helps to give form and substance to an entrepreneurial vision. The better the plan, the better equipped your company will be to recognize and take advantage of the opportunities that lie ahead. It can truly

mean the difference between success and failure. There are
sample business plans, some free, at your local library and
on the Internet. Some of the questions your business plan
should answer include:

1. What is my business plan?
2. What is my mission?
3. What are my services and/or products?
4. Who is my target audience?
5. Who are my competitors?
6. What is my marketing strategy?
7. How should I best utilize my resources?

And most importantly:

8. What is the profit potential?

*Remember, these can all develop with the progress of
your business.*

- You can turn to a variety of sources for financing of your
business. Savings accounts, family and friends, bank loans,
partners, shareholders, venture capitalists (very popular
with E-publishers), are all equal game to the entrepreneur.
A popular method that some small publishers are using is
the "Project Investment Scenario," where investors can
contribute capital to a specific book, and receive returns
from the sales of that book. This scenario works well for
both the publisher (who doesn't have to give up any of
his/her company), and the investor (who can "pick" and
"choose" attractive projects to invest in, even when the
overall company may not be of interest).

- Lastly, the value of maintaining good records is a necessary
part of doing continual business. We've all heard of the
businessman who lost his house, his car and his life's
savings, because his records weren't organized and he

failed to handle his tax responsibilities. The Federal Government regulations make it virtually impossible to avoid keeping detailed records. As I mentioned earlier, either secure financial accounting software, or hire an accountant to help you set up your books. It may not seem like a big deal now, but when you have orders for hundreds of books coming in each week, you'll be thanking me. An efficient system of record-keeping can help you to:

1. Monitor performance
2. Keep track of expenses
3. Track invoices
4. Protect your assets
5. Prepare your financial statements

And most importantly:

6. Keep the IRS off of your back.

The World of Publishing

The origins of book publishing can be traced to back to the Ancient World. As early as 600 B.C. scribes were known to have copied poems and speeches which they sold for high prices. According to Microsoft's *Encarta Encyclopedia*, Plato's students published and sold his lectures, and by about 250 B.C., Egypt had become one of the great book marts of the world by selling books through the Library of Alexandria, founded by Ptolemy I.

Much later in the New World, classics were published by the likes of Anne Bradstreet, Johnathan Edwards, Thomas Jefferson, Ben Franklin, Olaudah Equiano, Harriet Jacobs, David Walker, etc., all of whom published even before the late 1800's immigration of Europeans.

Of course, things have changed considerably, as the focus of publishing has shifted from a cultural emphasis to *the bottom line*. Publishing is now a $24 billion dollar a year business. Just think, if you just set your financial goals at one percent of one percent of this figure, you'd be a millionaire. *Twice*. There are plenty other companies that are trying to do exactly what you are doing. In fact, there are over 50,000 publishers in the United States. Some 60,000 books are published a year, according to industry estimates, a figure that reflects a steady rise for at least two decades. With the onslaught of mega-mergers and chain bookstores, competition for shelf-space and readers, especially amongst smaller publishers, has significantly heightened. So why would anyone attempt to do this himself or herself? It's simple. First, as the Internet becomes more popular, more distribution models and greater profit margins are available for even the smallest self-publisher; and second, if you have the knowledge, a little creativity, persistence, and learn *my* lessons well (in other words, you finish this book, and buy copies for 10 of your writer friends), book publishing can be both fun and rewarding. Sometimes you end up doing better as a small self-publisher than you might as a mid-list author at a large publishing house. On the other hand, the endeavor could be a disaster. Let's make sure you at least have the power to control your outcome.

There are numerous types of book publishers, including small presses, university presses, and vanity publishers (companies that charge you a fee to publish your book). Below, I have described two other types to help give you a thorough understanding of the types of publishers and where you may fit.

Commercial publishers or trade publishers are the large New York houses with which we are all familiar: Harper-Collins (Founded in 1817 as Harper Brothers), Little Brown & Company (Founded in 1837, now an imprint of Warner Books), Houghton-Mifflin (Founded in 1849), etc. Many of these companies are now owned by multi-national conglomerates, and are, therefore, more likely to primarily publish for profit. In fact, today, five major conglomerates control 80 percent of the book market. These publishers take the business/financial risk of publishing a manuscript for purposes of selling the finished product to the trade (distributors, wholesalers, bookstores), book clubs, subsidiary rights (film, audio book, foreign rights, etc.). Commercial publishers are mostly popular for two reasons: (1) they offer advances (up-front cash that is really a draw against your future sales) that average close to $10,000 (unless you're John Grisham or Anne Tyler and then you can add three or four more zeros to that number); and (2) they provide immediate credibility and media exposure for the budding author (not to mention global distribution).

Independent publishers, like commercial houses, assume the publishing risk, and may provide advances and media exposure. The primary difference is that these companies are comprised mainly of publishers, editors, and salespeople who may have been intellectually disenfranchised by (and probably psychologically disenchanted with) their former bosses (at the New York houses), and have since left. Independents are most often owned by the employees, as in the case of W.W. Norton, Walter Mosley's publisher; or non-profits, as in The New Press (which, of course, is run by a former Random House executive). While the New York houses are "commercial" in their content and focus, the independents practice a form of publishing that is intellectually and often politically engaging.

Publishing Made Easy

You are not alone in this journey. You join hundreds of other self-publishers who have enjoyed some modicum of success (well, at least recognition). Edgar Allen Poe, Henry David Thoreau, Spencer Johnson, James Redfield, Omar Tyree, and Richard Paul Evans (of *The Christmas Box* fame) are just a few names to inspire you. There are some minor details that you need to attend to in order to make your book business legitimate. I know you're ready to get back to the creative work, but remember writing is an art; *publishing is a business.*

• An ISBN number is a worldwide identification system for published books. It's like a social security number for your work. It stands for International Standard Book Number, and you can secure it from the agency that governs and issues them, R.R. Bowker (www.bowker.com). After filling out an ISBN application, Bowker will issue you a listing of ISBN numbers in increments of 10, 100 and 1000, depending on how many titles you plan to publish. Of course, the cost increases with each increment. Once you get your listing, you will select a number for your first book, and this number will appear on the copyright page of your book, as well as on the barcode that is incorporated on the back of your book (see Step 4). Bookstores and libraries around the international marketplace stay abreast of new titles and place orders using Bowker's "Books In Print" ISBN database.

You can now obtain your ISBN number and applications online at http://www.bowker.com/standards/

- About four months before you plan to print your book, apply to participate in the Library of Congress Card Number Program (LCCN) and the Library of Congress Cataloging in Publication Data Program (CIP). Both offices are the same, but the programs are mutually exclusive. Your title will be eligible for one or the other. This can also be done online. I have found that both of these services have to rank among the most efficient provided by any bureaucracy in the United States, as the response time is one week, and both services are *free*. If you want to sell to libraries (and you should, as they buy *muchos libros*) a Library of Congress Card Number is mandatory.

- Once you complete your book and sign your name, it is copyright protected by law. The next step is to have your copyright registered. You can do this by filling out and sending in the appropriate applications to the copyright department within the Library of Congress. Don't forget to print the copyright symbol on the copyright page of your book. You can find instructions, as well as, more information on LOC numbers at http://www.loc.gov/.

- Develop a budget for your book-publishing project early. You will have to determine your expenses and project your revenue, and then determine what your profits should be. From your expenses, you will also be able to determine what the price of your book (list price) will be. I usually look at prices of similar type books, in size, look, feel and content, and then examine my unit cost of each book. After this exploration, the numbers tell me what the list price should be. Please know that most books never make a profit on the first printing, as you have so many one-time expenses to recover, such as editing.

Pricing your book is very important; it is one way that you position your book for profit. A general rule of thumb is that the book should sell for three to five times the first-run production costs, but what the market will bear has to also be considered. The first run should generally be no more than what you think you can successfully sell in a year. *The book budget sample is on page 33.*

Now that you are a Publisher, it's time to get informed on a more personal level. A subscription to related periodicals such as *Publisher's Weekly, Small Press*, and *New York Times Book Review*, will keep you abreast of the major players and plays in publishing. Joining literary and publishing organizations will keep you in the book "loop." Writers' conferences and industry conferences will allow you to interact with like-minded individuals as well as introduce you to new and cutting edge ideas and technologies. Each June, The American Booksellers Association presents Book Exposition of America (BEA), the largest industry gathering of publishing professionals in the world. In addition, they host regional conferences throughout the year. Attending these types of events will help you get the word out on your new company, collect orders, acquire new information, and make deals. Remember that publishing is predicated on content, and even though you are self-publishing, selling subsidiary rights (Foreign publication, film, etc.) can be very lucrative. A few years ago while attending the BEA, I was approached by a German Publisher who wanted to purchase the German publication rights to a pulp novel that I published. The

That Guy had spent a great deal of money on *The Book*, yet had no idea how much. I put together the following simple budget for him:

The Book Budget
Projected Expenses

Administrative	$ 500.00
*Editorial	$ 300.00
(That Guy had a friend who was an English Professor)	
*Book Design/Layout	$ 250.00
(Another friend)	
Printing/Shipping (1000 copies)	$ 3,000.00
*Marketing	$ 4,000.00
*Miscellaneous	$ 1,000.00
Total Expenses:	$ 9,050.00
Unit Cost (per book)	$9.05

*One-time costs not a factor on second printing

Projected Revenue
Book Sales
(1000 books: 75% at Wholesale discounted rate of $6, 25% at List/Retail price of $15) $10,250.00

Projected Net Profit   **$1,200.00**

After seeing this, *That Guy* decided to increase the print run from 1000 to 3000 books, and increase the price of The Book from $15 to $15.95, in an effort to increase his net profit.

money was not immense but the exposure and literary credibility was unmatchable. There are numerous other rights such as audio books and mass market (the small books you see in the grocery store checkout line) from which self-published authors can reap big rewards.

Many online literary and publishing organizations offer free information and professional advice. Doing a search on any search engine will list thousands of these resources.

Self-publishing is first and foremost a business. Learning as much as you can now about the business of books will make your work that much easier when you're dealing with bookstores, media and other people you will need to convince that you are deserving of their support and partnering. The more credible the business person, the easier your path to success will be.

The tasks I've shared in this step are the foundation for the entrepreneurial ride ahead. Clear this work out of your way, with careful attention, and the ride won't be bumpy at all.

Worksheet 3:
Building a Business

1. Choose three possible names for your business. List them here.

   a) _____

   b) _____

   c) _____

   Ask ten people to rank your names in order of most appealing to least appealing. Then choose the one you really like.

2. Flesh out your business plan.

   What is the mission of your business? Why do you want to do this? What services/products do you intend to offer? How are you going to sell/market those products? How are you going to finance your business? Make a note of cash on hand that you can spend, sources of other capital and loans.

   _____

   _____

3. What will your logo look like? Choose something that goes with the name, even if only in your mind. Then, unless you are artistically talented, hire a graphic designer to design your corporate identity.

4. Determine the list price of your book. Write your projected production costs, following the example given earlier.

   _____

   _____

5. Now, go to the bookstore and bench-mark. Study the books that you find attractive. Make a note of the number of pages, price, binding, layout of the book, and the cover. Record that information.

   _____

   _____

Selected Reading

Epstein, Jason. *Book Business: Publishing: Past, Present, and Future.* New York: W. W. Norton & Company, 2001.

Godin, Seth. *The Bootstrapper's Bible: How to start and build a business with a great idea and (almost) no money.* Upstart Publishing, 1998.

Hart, James. *The Popular Book: A History of America's Literary Trade.* Oxford University Press, 1950.

Kamoroff, Bernard B. *Small Time Operator: How to Start Your Own Business, Keep Your Books, Pay Your Taxes, and Stay Out of Trouble.* Bell Springs Publications, 2001.

Norman, Jan. *What No One Ever Tells You About Starting Your Own Business: Real Life Start-Up Advice from 101 Successful Entrepreneurs.* Upstart Publishing Company, 1999.

Pinson, Linda. *Keeping the Books: Basic Recordkeeping and Accounting for the Successful Small Business.* Upstart Publishing Company, 1998.

Poynter, Dan. *Self-Publishing Manual: How to Write, Print and Sell your own Book (Revised).* California: Para Publishing, 1997.

Ross, Marilyn and Tom Ross *The Complete Guide to Self-Publishing.* (Revised) Writer's Digest Books, 2002.

Salisbury, Linda and Joy. *Smart Publishing.* Tabby House, 1997.

Schriffin, Andre. *The Business of Books: How the International Conglomerates Took Over Publishing and Changed the Way We Read.* Verso Books, 2000.

Woll, Thomas. *Publishing for Profit: Successful Bottom-Line Management for Book Publishers.* Fisher Books, 1998.

Woll, Thomas. *Selling Subsidiary Rights: An Insider's Guide.* Fisher Books, 1998.

Step 4.

Creating a Masterpiece:
Designing Your Product

Step 4. Creating a Masterpiece:
Designing Your Product

Like most people, you probably do judge a book by its cover. If the cover is unattractive, the chances of you buying it are highly unlikely. In this commercial age, where publishers are allotting hundreds of thousands of dollars for book tours, print ads and heavy marketing, your cover becomes your preeminent sales tool. Most of us can't compete with the big ad budgets, but you can design a product that looks professional, entices readers, and visually stands out in front of the pack. Deciding on the right colors, photos, and placement of text, are all part of the design decision-making process. Who wants to buy the used gray bike in the dusty corner of the store, when the brand new, shiny, red ten-speed hangs in the window (on sale)? In this step, your creative/business balance will be tested. The design is the first element of your book that is solely customer-centric. If you build it (and it looks good), they will come.

Graphic Design, Desktop Publishing and Typesetting

Graphic Arts is the profession involving the application of lines, strokes and images to a two-dimensional surface. Every time we see the huge ad on the side of a city bus, or an ad for Volkswagen in O (okay, that's my last Oprah plug, *promise*), we are seeing the work of graphic artists. Before we decide whether we want to farm out the design work or do it ourselves, let's explore the different types of graphic arts.

- Graphic design is the general term for artists who use computers to create and manipulate images and text to create some visual product. Whether it be a newspaper ad, letterhead, or a book cover, graphic designers spend endless hours coming up with visual ideas. Software programs that designers typically use include: Adobe Photoshop, Corel Draw, Adobe Illustrator, and Quark Xpress.

- Desktop publishing and typesetting mean essentially the same thing. Both are concerned with the formatting and layout (or page composition) of text on a page. Each deals with the production of documents—sometimes lengthy, like textbooks. In the case of book production, often the desktop publisher will take the template that the graphic designer has created for the cover, and use it to layout and format the text (commonly referred to as "guts"). Software programs that designers typically use include:

Quark Xpress, Pagemaker, and very rarely Word Perfect or Microsoft Word.

In-house or Freelancers

If you have the time, energy, skill, desire, hardware and software, it may prove easier for you to design the book yourself. On the other hand, you may not want the responsibility of creating a book design that will consistently attract readers. I have consulted with several writers over the years who have completely left the design phase to a freelancer, while others have engaged in a more hands-on approach.

If indeed you plan to hire out, keep in mind that you are looking for a book designer, not simply a graphic designer. You will need a professional who has experience in designing and laying out books. Of course, that's easier said than done, as most of the country's book designers are in New York, the publishing capital of the world. Check with your writer's league. The easiest way around this is to know what you want and convey that to your freelancer. Let's look at what it is you want and how much it should cost you:

- You want a graphic designer who knows the element of book cover design. This can range from $30/hour to $100/hour, or you can negotiate a flat fee if the freelancer is open to that. In 1999, I negotiated a book cover design for a flat fee of $800. In contrast, a year prior I paid a handsome $1200 for a cover that was billed at $45/hour.
- You want a desktop publisher who knows how to layout and format pages and chapters of text. The rates are primarily the same as a graphic designer.

NOTE: Try to find a designer who can do both your cover and "guts." This will save you time and money.

Contract with the designer to provide you with two to three sample design templates for your cover and text. After viewing the different options, go with one that you feel confident about (and the one that looks the best). This is another good place to ask the opinions of people you trust in your own "focus group." Give the designer clear and concise direction, and you will be on your way to creating your masterpiece.

If you don't want to spend the money, and you have a MAC or IBM desktop computer (and the talent), designing your book can be a very exciting and professionally satisfying experience. Learn some of the design and desktop publishing programs I mentioned earlier. They each have book layout functions that are automated and thus feasible for the learned novice. If you know nothing about book design, my first suggestion is to visit your local bookstore.

In 1996 when I started production on a educational Textbook by a local writer, I visited the local Borders Books and Music Store. I camped out in the education, and children's lit sections for what seemed like days. I looked at every book that remotely resembled my client's manuscript, paying attention to similarities among these works in artwork, size, binding, photo placement, spine and so much more. By the time I left Borders I knew exactly what I wanted the cover to look like. I highly recommend this exercise to writers, self-publishers and graphic designers in my seminar. RESEARCH! Look at hundreds of covers and guts. Find out what you like, what you don't like, and what your resources will allow you to utilize. While you may want a comment from Stephen King on the front of your horror novel, the chances are pretty slim that you will get it. One from Thomas

Sanders might be more feasible. Who's Tom Sanders, you say? That's my point!

My second suggestion is to sketch out what you want. Take a notebook with you on your research trip. No need to be Leroy Campbell or Picasso, just a basic idea of what you want will suffice.

Third, become familiar with the elements of good book design. Let's discuss that further.

Color, Images, and Photographs

Choosing the right look for your cover is a challenging task. It must be a selling tool, so make it distinctive and intriguing to the eye. A cover that has colors will add a multi-dimensional effect, while a cover with black text on white projects little. Once you become famous like Dean Koontz or Deepak Chopra, you could probably get away with no color. Consider the use of artwork or photography on your cover. Depending on what you discover in your research, one may work better than the other. You can get images for your cover in a variety of ways. Choose a stock photograph or clip art. Better yet, hire an artist to paint an original work for your cover. Find out what images other similar books use on their covers, and make yours better.

The Book was a contemporary romance novel, so it belonged to a family of fiction with bright-colored covers, sexy portraits and slick scenes. We visited a bookstore, where I chose ten books that were similar in size, shape and theme, and showed them to **That Guy**. He liked none of them. As we walked out of the bookstore, **That Guy** noticed a postcard with a painting he really liked. He instantly decided it would look good on his book cover.

Unfortunately, the painting was a well-known piece of art, which meant that licensing it was almost impossible, since he did not have six figures to drop. So we did the next best thing. We hired an artist to paint a similar scene. It was very formulaic, but his motivation was to create a cover that completely represented the story. The designer, a friend of the author, did exactly that, and it looked great.

Your front cover should consist of:

1. Title *(Do The Write Thing)*
2. Subtitle, if you have one. *(7 Steps to Publishing Success)*
3. Author's Name (Kwame Alexander with Nina Foxx)
4. Logo of Publishing Company (Optional: Some companies do this, like Penguin Putnam)
5. Blurb (Blurbs are comments in support of the book usually on the back cover. Typically, if you have a really great one, like Alice Walker or the *New York Times*, you will place it on the front to garner attention.)

Your back cover should consist of:

- Title
- Blurbs or endorsements of the book
- Summary of book (Once again, optional)
- Author photo (This can make or break you, so look your best.)
- Logo, Name of Publishing Company
- Price (Typically, U.S. & Canada)
- Bar-Code (A bar code is a series of vertical lines in a white box that can be scanned for price and other information)
- You may want to include credits on the back cover. An example would be:
  Cover Design: Kim Greyer Graphic Design

Your spine (or the side of your book) should consist of:

1. Author Name
2. Title
3. Company Logo or Name

The spine should make a splashing visual statement, so when it is placed on the bookshelf, spine out, as most books are, the color and title will attract the attention of browsers.

Since we've already discussed the front matter, body and back matter, let's move on to a discussion of production processes.

What are A Pages?

Production is the phase of your book that comes right after you've made your last edits, and right before you send it to the printer. Some like to call it post-final rewrite, or pre-blueline. With a proper understanding of the design process, you can now develop the production schedule, which delineates the last mile of your course (See Appendix A). The A Pages are the first set of page comps (page composition or text that has been completely formatted) from the designer. You will then check for problems with formatting, inconsistencies and other things that you, the author, would notice easily. You will give the A pages back to the designer, and after your changes are made, you will then receive the B pages from the designer. Your copyeditor (or friend with an English degree) will then review, proofread the manuscript for grammar, punctuation and typos, and return it to you. Before returning it to the designer, you will check to make sure you want to accept the changes the copyeditor made. Once the designer has made these changes, you will receive the Final pages. The copyeditor will then check once more before you examine it, and the designer makes final changes.

It never hurts to let a few people do a "clean-eyes," or read-through of your completed manuscript quickly. Skipping a few of these steps can lead to unnecessary mistakes later in the production process.

The first thing we notice about a book is the cover. If it's a good cover, we may look at the back. If it's a great cover, we will glance inside. The goal is to create a visually appealing book, inside and out, that will allow us to find out about the treasure that exists between your covers (That didn't come out right, but I think you get the point).

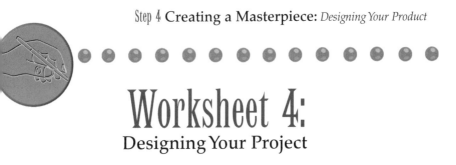

Worksheet 4:
Designing Your Project

1. Now is a good time to set a benchmark, paying attention to book covers that catch your eye. You can do this in a local bookstore, and you can even begin online at any e-bookstore. Make a list of three titles that catch your eye, noting the main colors in the cover, plus anything else you find appealing. Don't forget to indicate whether they use original art or simply graphic elements.

   Title 1: _____

   _____

   _____

   Title 2: _____

   _____

   _____

   Title 3: _____

   _____

   _____

2. Brainstorm for the names of some people who you might ask to give you a blurb for your back cover. Research where you might contact these people. Write their names and contact information here.

   a) _____

   _____

   b) _____

   _____

   c) _____

   _____

3. If you have decided to include a photograph on your cover, decide
what type of image you want to project and how you might do that.
Do you want to appear friendly? Knowledgeable? Welcoming? Write
down the names of some places where you might be able to secure
an inexpensive photographer. Some sources might be photography or
art schools or referrals.

Selected Reading

Adobe Creative Team. *Adobe Photoshop 5.0 Classroom in a Book.*
Adobe Press, 1998.

Parker, Roger C. and Patrick Berry. *Looking Good in Print (4th Ed).*
Ventana Press, 1990.

Parker, Roger C. *Desktop Publishing & Design For Dummies®.*
Hungry Minds, Inc. 1995.

Pretzer, Mary. *Creative Low-Budget Publication Design.*
North Light Books, 1999.

Supon Design Group. *Breaking the Rules in Publication Design.*
Madison Square Press, 2001.

Weinmann, Elaine. *Quark XPress™ 4 for Macintosh:*
Visual QuickStart Guide. Peachpit Press, 1997.

Weinmann, Elaine and Corbin Collins. *Quark XPress 4 for Windows:*
Visual QuickStart Guide. Peachpit Press, 1998.

Williams, Robin. *The Non-Designer's Design Book.*
Peachpit Press, 1994.

Step 5.

Putting It Together:
Printing Your Book

Step 5. Putting It Together:
Printing Your Book

If I were to ask you if you wanted to print your cover in four-color process, or four PMS colors, what would your answer be? You probably didn't know that it costs about the same most of the time. Printers are a lot like auto mechanics. If you don't have a basic working knowledge of the terminology and processes, you *will* be taken. Do your homework. (Reading this book is a good start.)

It is not always an intentional thing, but printers are in business to make money, and they want customers to buy as many of their services as possible. In addition, most authors think that the printing process is the most complicated and expensive part of the publishing process. It is my intention to show you in Step 5, that it is actually the complete opposite. Before we delve into this process, let's take a look at an exciting new technology that makes book manufacturing cheaper, easier and more accessible.

What is an eBook?

An eBook is a special computer file which contains the text of a printed book. The file may be read on a personal computer (PC), a personal digital assistant (PDA), or an electronic device designed specifically for reading eBooks (eBook reader).

When I began writing this book our society was firmly established in the Digital Age. Thus, I knew that I would focus some of my efforts on the new electronic book technologies. Troy Johnson, a friend and webmaster of aalbc.com, supplied me with the above eBook definition. He believes that eBooks may radically change the way we read, disseminate information, and even define our culture. I am not completely sold, but he has done extensive research and makes a strong case for the ebook option. He writes:

> "With eBooks the cost of book publishing is greatly reduced. One simply has to take the text of a book and convert it into a format useable by an eBook reader. The cost of storage and distribution is negligible. An eBook is simply data stored on a computer.
>
> The only risk associated with authoring an eBook is the time invested in writing it. Today most authors write their books on computers. An eBook can be generated from the original document on the computer in a few minutes. The resulting file may be uploaded to an eBook retailer (such as Fatbrain.com) for immediate availability on-line.

The publication decision is left entirely up to the author. The risk to the reader is less for two major reasons: (1) eBook versions of a book cost less than their paper based counterpart, and (2) typically readers are allowed to download, for free, a chapter or more of the book to read at their leisure. Unlike the trailer for a movie, this is an actual sample of the book, not just the highlights. The reader gets a chance to read the author's material and make a determination of whether or not it will satisfy their need. This is happening today; on-line booksellers provide excerpts (essentially eBook excerpts) for their on-line customers.

One might argue that the current publishing process helps screen out bad books by preventing them from reaching the marketplace. The publishing industry is currently rife with stories of excellent books that can't get published and poor ones that do. Publication of eBooks moves the publication decision from the publisher to the author. As a result, the reader is allowed to read, not what the publisher decides to publish, but what the author decides to write."

It is not likely that eBooks will supplant books as the primary reading platform. We can utilize some of the strategies to enhance our printing and publishing goals.

Getting Ready to Print?

When your designer has completed inputting the final edits, you will receive a disk with the book cover and guts. This disk will eventually go to the printer. But first, you need to choose a printer. Looking in a printing magazine such as *Book Tech*, or searching the Internet, will provide you with several options. I suggest selecting three to four potential book printers. Stay away from local printers for one main reason: they are not book printers. Thus, their presses (printing machines) are not set up to print books, which means you will be paying significantly more money.

I know a guy who printed his book of essays with a local printer that specialized in business cards and the like. He ended up paying $1500 for one hundred books. That's fifteen dollars per book for printing alone. He sold the book for thirty dollars. Needless to say, not too many people purchased it.

Once you have chosen the printers, you will need to send them specification sheets (so you need to have one completed).

A spec sheet (see example in Appendix B) includes a list of all the vital information that the printer will need to give you a printing estimate:

- *Page Count.* Count every page in your book towards the final page count. Page counts typically should correspond with the signatures that the printers use. A signature is a group of pages printed at one time. If the printer prints on eight pages signatures, your page count should be divisible by eight (not including the cover).

- *Quantity.* The break-even point for book printing is typically 1000 books. In order to get the best price for your book, you will need to print in increments of 1000. Of course, the more copies you print, the better unit cost you will have.

- *Trim Size:* Most printers can accommodate any size you want but there are standard sizes that utilize the paper better and cost less. Some of the most common sizes are 5.5 x 8.5, 6 x 9, 8.5 x 11. The benchmark you set earlier will come in handy in helping you determine this.

- *Paper Stock.* There are many types of cover and text paper from which to choose. Ask each of the printers to send you cover and text samples, and try to think about what will look most appealing to the people who will buy your book. As an example, most paperback books have covers that are 10 or 12pt (point represents the thickness of stock) coated one side (C1S). An example of a type of text paper is 50 pound (pound represents the weight of the paper) white offset. The range of colors and feel is immense and warrants some research.
- *Binding.* There are several types of binding that will give your the book the professional look it needs and deserves:
  1. *Case bound:* a cloth hardback book with a hard or stiff cover?
  2. *Perfect bound:* a paperback book in which all of the pages are trimmed at the edge and glued together.
  3. *Saddle Stitch:* a paperback book in which pages are inserted into sections then fastened together with two staples through the middle fold of the sheets.
  4. *Other forms of binding* are Plastic-coil, Xerox Thermal, and GBC. Perfect bound and Casebound are the two most common binding types preferred in stores, libraries and other outlets.
- *Ink.* Your printer will need to know how many colors you have on your cover and in your guts. Typically, you will have a two, four or six-color cover, and black and white text. The Pantone Matching System (PMS) is an industry standard that is recognized by designers, publishers and printers worldwide. Whenever you decide on a color, you will need to refer to the PMS number. You can visit www.pantone.com for more details.

- *Art.* This refers to how you will provide the book to the printer. Will it be camera-ready (laser printout) or a digital file (on a zip disk)?
- *Proof.* A blueline is a photoprint (with blue ink) of the "guts" of your book, made from stripped-up negatives or positives, and used to check the position of the elements of your book and verify the page numbering. They must be approved quickly and returned to the printer to stay on the production schedule. A matchprint is a photographic print of a four-color cover used to check the accuracy of the colors to be printed.

Once you have all this information, you will put it on the spec sheet and send it to the selected printers. In time, you will receive quotes from each of the printers indicating the cost of the job and the optimum delivery date. Based on the quotes, you will choose the printer for your book. It's usually a good rule of thumb to let the other bidders know that they were not chosen, as you may choose (or need) to work with them in the future. As a general rule of thumb, bids are only valid for thirty days to reflect sudden paper and printing cost shifts in the market.

Printing prices are very competitive, and with the proper research you will be able to find an affordable price well within your budget. Remember, the more copies you print, the less your cost. Conversely, the less you print, the more your cost will increase. Learn the printing lingo so that you can properly convey your needs and expectations.

Around the time that we were ready to print *The Book*, Xerox was introducing it's new Docutech Print-on-Demand Technology (I will discuss this in detail later). As I mentioned earlier, we skipped the copyediting phase, printed one laser copy and prepared our disk to send to the printer. On the way to the printer, I just happened to glance at the manuscript and immediately noticed three errors on the first page. Unfortunately, *That Guy* demanded that we forge ahead.

The Book was a 6" x 9" book of 300 pages with a four-color cover, and we printed 2000 copies. The total cost was $4000, for a unit printing cost of two dollars per book. When we received the printed books six weeks later, our eyes lit up with pleasant satisfaction. The cover was colorful, glossy and very attractive. A few months later, as *The Book* made it to bookstores around the country, *That Guy* and I started receiving emails and calls from friends, readers, strangers, booksellers, and enemies.

One caller said "I found 147 typos in your book." A reviewer wrote, "It might have been a good book, if I'd finished it. I stopped after the 13th misspelled word." What made matters worse is that it was a pretty good book (with a fantastic cover).

Two things happened after the mass error discovery. One, bookstores were selling out in record time and needed books as soon as possible to fill the demand. That was a plus. We had not even thought about reprinting. Two, **_That Guy_** realized that we'd better let a copyeditor read **_The Book_**. Usually your printing price decreases significantly on reprints, because you are using the same plates. We were supplying a new, corrected disk, and so our cost was going nowhere. Once we had a corrected book, we opted to print on Docutech technology, which took six days, as opposed to the book printer's six weeks. We began printing five hundred books a week. This worked well for our immediate needs, but at a cost of five dollars per book. Two lessons you can learn from our mistakes:

1. Always PROOF, before the book goes to the printer. SAVE MONEY!
2. Always track your Book's sales, so you can plan better for reprints. SAVE MONEY!

Preparing Your Book for the Printer

Providing a camera-ready copy of your book was the norm in the past. In the electronic information age, a digital file (on disk or via email or FTP) is desired for the best output. The first time you try to submit digitally, give yourself enough time in case of errors in transfer.

The first step is to ask the printer exactly how s/he would like the text and cover files submitted. This will save you time and headache. The printer may want you to save or embed the fonts (it's easier than it sounds). If there are photos or artwork, you may want the printer to scan them for higher resolution. The advantage to using a digital file, is that the printer will be using the first generation of your book to generate printing plates, rather than a second generation from a laser printout.

Different Printing Models

The best bridge between the markets of today and the technologies of tomorrow, Print-on-demand or digital printing is constantly in the headlines today. It was designed to be the new printing model for smaller publishers, and large publishers with out-of-print and mid-list books. Xerox pioneered on-demand technology with the Docutech high speed copier. They promised short runs, low cost and fast turnarounds. With the Docutech, you no longer had to print thousands of books and store them in your basement to collect dust. You could print ten, or fifty at a time, based on demand and save money on storage and fulfillment. The cost of on-demand is not as competitive as long-run book printing. Whether you are printing ten or a hundred books, there is no quantity discount. If you are planning to use a Docutech, your documents should be converted into Adobe Acrobat (PDF) or postscript format for printing (Docutech will print from your digital file, as opposed to placing originals on glass or in feeder).

The majority of book printing in this country is done by offset and/or sheetfed printers. Sheetfed printers specialize in printing 2000 or less books. With standard trim sizes of 5.5 x 8.5, these presses print sheets with thirty-two to 128 pages. The inking systems evenly distribute the ink on both sides of the sheet. The sheets then go to large folders that form them into signatures of at least thirty-two pages. The automated binders then gather the signatures, glue them together, and trim, all in one pass. Web offset presses print on rolls of paper, which are cheaper than the sheets, and at the end of the press run, it delivers a folded signature, rather than a flat sheet, thus consolidating the two processes. With over 25,000 impressions per hour, offset is the most economical when printing more than 3000 copies. The advantages of a web press are speed and low cost.

There is nothing greater than receiving your books from the printer. Give yourself a pat on the back, take a breather, and gear up to pull some late nights. Now that we have the books, we have to step up our marketing efforts.

Worksheet 5:
Printing Your Book

1. Prepare your spec sheet

    *   Number of pages: *(Add pages if necessary to make this number divisible by 8. Be sure to include your front and back matter.)*

    *   Number you want to print: (How much can you afford?)
        Get quotes for the number you decide on plus at least two other quantities, e.g. 1000, 2000, and 3000.

    *   What size will your book be? Your benchmark will come in handy again. What size are similar books? What fits on the shelf nicely?

    *   What type paper? White? Cream? Fuschia? What weight?
        (This book is on 80# paper.)

    *   What type binding?

    *   What inks will you use for the cover? Guts? Keep in mind that pictures inside your book may make it more expensive to produce.

    *   How will you need to supply files? This may depend on your printer. Check out the different types and make sure you have the capability or can find someone to convert the files for you.

2. Get printing quotes. Make sure you get at least five quotes your first time out. Prices vary widely. Don't be afraid to ask for references and samples.

    _____

    _____

    _____

    _____

    _____

    _____

3. Brainstorm about ways you use ebook strategies to augment your printing and publishing goals. Write some of those ideas here.

_____

_____

_____

_____

_____

Selected Reading

Adobe Creative Team. *Adobe Acrobat 5.0*. Adobe Press, 2001.

Allen, Roger MacBride. *A Quick Guide to Book-On-Demand Printing: Learn How to Print and Bind Your Own Paperback Books.* Foxacre Press, 2000.

Beach, Mark and Eric Kenly. *Getting It Printed: How to Work With Printers and Graphic Imaging Services to Assure Quality, Stay on Schedule and Control Costs*. North Light Books, 1999.

Brenni, Vito Joseph. *Book Printing in Britain and America*. Greenwood Publishing Group, 1983.

Cohen, Sandee. *The Non-Designer's Scan and Print Book*. Peachpit Press, 1999.

Cost, Frank. *Pocket Guide to Digital Printing*. Delmar Publishers, 1995.

Craig, James. *Production for the Graphic Designer*. Watson-Guptill Publications, 1990.

Kursmark, Louise. *How to Start a Home-Based Desktop Publishing Business*. Globe Pequot Press, 1999.

Romano, Frank J. *Pocket Guide to Digital Prepress*. Delmar Publishers, 1995.

Step 6.

Promoting Yourself:
Marketing Your Book

Step 6. Promoting Yourself:
Marketing Your Book

You might have written the great American novel, but if no one knows about it, it can't sell. Marketing your book is almost as important as designing the cover. It starts from day one and is an on-going process throughout the life of your book. Just because this happens to be step six, it doesn't mean you start here. Hopefully, you started promoting and advertising your masterpiece some time ago.

Marketing is the process by which you let others know you have a product for sale. Publicity (free marketing) and advertising (paid marketing) are different forms of marketing. Marketing is how you create a demand. Your goal in marketing is to make people want to do business with you and buy your book. In essence, when you first started telling people that you wrote a book and it would be published on a specific date, you were marketing. But, unless you only plan to sell your books out of the trunk of your car, you need to go beyond just word of mouth with your immediate family and friends.

Be goal directed. By now, you have developed a concept for your book. Decide how you are going to market it to your intended audience. Write a general marketing plan to go along with the business plan you wrote earlier. (You did, didn't you?).

Writing a Marketing Plan

How are you going to let people know about your book? Are you going to tell all your friends? Does your title or subject lend itself to any creative marketing ideas? One author I knew wrote a book on financial planning, and had postcards printed that looked like dollar bills on one side. (Thank goodness he didn't print both sides.) The information about his book was on the back.

To write an effective marketing plan, you need to know your publishing business, what types of books compete with yours, and why someone should buy your book over another. You also must consider the opportunities for selling your book, and who might be the most interested in it. This will tell you who your primary target is.

Establish your marketing goals to capitalize on your strengths and minimize your weaknesses. Remember that marketing is a process and you will have to change this plan along with the changes in your market if you want to keep selling books. With this basic information, you can come up with marketing objectives and action steps for selling your book over a year's time.

Don't think you have to spend a lot of money to come up with a successful marketing plan, either. There are many free or inexpensive avenues you can take before you even spend one dime (or at least a whole lot of dimes on things like paid advertisement), such as friends and family (and other people you might have passed on the street).

Compile all of your personal addresses and mailing lists. This means family, friends, friends of family and friends, business associates any one else you can think of. Make note of all organizations with which you are affiliated. If it is possible, computerize these and make labels. Trust me, this may seem like an extra step, but if you plan to ever do this again, it will save you tons of time. Compose an attractive letter (or letters) that asks these people to buy copies or advance copies of your book. You might even offer them a discount if they buy before your book is actually published (this is called a "pre-publication discount"). This is a nice way to generate advance capital for your business, but please don't forget to fill the orders once the book is published (good record-keeping is a life-saver).

Writing a Press Kit

Your marketing plan should include the development of a press kit. Make it professional. Many bookstore owners and media outlets will be using it to make decisions that can affect your book sales, such as scheduling book signings or even recommending your book to customers. Your local independent bookstore owner will probably have seen lots of them and might be willing to share with you pieces of press kits they still have around. Look at them. See what is included in the kits that appeal to you most. Make sure yours is reproduced on a nice quality paper. In the beginning, you may not have a lot in your press kit, but as time goes on, and you get numerous print mentions and interviews, you will be able to add to it. The basic elements should be:

- A well written press release about your new book
- Ordering information-How do people order the book? Make sure you do some research about discounts.
- A professional looking author photo
- Your biography
- An interview with the author
- Your tour schedule
- If your book is non-fiction, a table of contents
- Your book cover (We all know it's fabulous, so this alone is going to make people want your book, right?)
- Any promotional items - A postcard, a bookmark, etc. Now is a good time to decide if your book lends itself to any type of promotional ideas like those mentioned earlier. You might want to include these in your press kit.

The press kit will help you generate orders from bookstores and distributors, or secure book signings and media interviews that will help you generate orders. Visit local bookstores and make sure the right person (usually the Publicist, Community Relations Coordinator, or Manager) has a copy of your press kit. Send copies to book review editors at your local newspapers. Let them know you are available for interview. Research online. Send e-mails to book clubs about your book. Some will request a copy of your press kit.

Dealing with the Media

While you are blanketing the world with your press kit and promotional materials, prepare yourself for numerous return calls and emails from the media. What are you going to say about your book? You want to sound like an authority on your subject. Prepare two or three short "pitches" about your book. Practice (in a mirror, with a friend or on a tape recorder). What if you get a television interview? It is not impossible, especially in your hometown. How are you going to dress? What type of image do you want to project? Think about these things in advance so that when The Today Show calls you can concentrate on the interview and not on what you are going to wear or how you will look. You don't get a second chance to make a first impression and compel people to run out and buy your book.

Book Signings

Book signings and readings are invaluable to the success of your publishing career. People are more apt to buy books by unknown authors when they get the opportunity to meet, greet and hear the author. Everybody you meet at one of these knows at least one person they can tell about your book, so preparing for book signings and treating them seriously goes a long way, even if you only sign books at your local church or in your hometown. (Don't laugh, book signings or events outside of bookstores can sell a lot of books.)

When bookstores see your stunning press kit, and call to schedule signings, what are you going to say? Develop a general script and keep it posted on the wall near your phone. If your press kit is good, they may remember you when you call and it will be easier. Some may ask for a review copy of your book first. Send it with a note and follow-up promptly. Receiving a book signing confirmation from a bookstore is similar to racing by your house, one han on the handlebars, the other waving to your mother, who is standing on the front porch with a great, big smile. It's a validation of all the work you have accomplished. There is a sample book signing timeline in Appendix D.

Once your book signing is planned, how will it go? Will have a formal format where you talk for a specified amount of time, answer questions and then sign books? Or will the signing be informal with people just wandering by? In eithe case, you have to know what you are going to say to convince people to buy your book.

Book signings, friends and media exposure are not the only opportunities you will have to market your book. Ther are many avenues on-line and elsewhere. Send press release Volunteer to speak at events. Sponsor things. Leave postcarc with the check at restaurants. Be creative. You will be surprised how people find out about you and your book.

A Word about using The Web

Should you or should you not use the web in promoting you book? How can you afford not to? There are a myriad of websites that book lovers frequent where you can list your book, often for free. You can also look up the websites of book clubs and others that might be interested and send the information about your book. You may even consider your own personal website that has details about your book and about you. It can be fashioned after your press kit and contain links to other writers. In turn, they will often swap links with you. You may even want to explore the possibility of your own cart, where people can buy directly from you, or at least find out where your book is available. You can point them to some of the on-line book retailers, such as Amazon.com and Barnes and Noble. If nothing else, you can direct people to your website for information about your book using a no-pressure scenario. A well-designed web site can increase your sales. Be sure to include a counter so that you can track your traffic.

In sum, publishing guru, Dan Poynter, echoes the necessary marketing mentality:

> *"Go into a bookstore on any given day. How many of the customers do you suppose are interested in a SCUBA book? Not many. What is the profile of the bookstore browser? It is the 'recreational reader,' someone used to plunking down $24.95 for hard-cover fiction. But check out a dive shop and how many customers are interested in a book on SCUBA? Now the thinking-gears are turning."*

The point is that almost every book has special appeal to certain readers. You need to find those readers, and let them know about your book.

For all the advance marketing and preparation *That Guy* had done, he had no clue how to "work a crowd." I mean, this guy was the most boring public speaker on earth. (Imagine Ross Perot delivering a sermon.) How was *That Guy* expecting to sell any books if no one stuck around during his readings? I decided to do two things. First, we did some media and PR training with him. Secondly, and simultaneously, we hired an actress and gave her a script of the first chapter of *The Book*. She memorized the script, developed the character and was ready. To do what you ask?

At the first book signing, where eighty people showed up (due to some of the techniques discussed in this step), *That Guy* started reading from the first chapter. I can still hear the yawns. Midway through the first paragraph, as instructed, the actress rose out of the audience, and began acting the script. She literally began to perform. The author stopped reading, and he, along with the stunned audience, listened and watched intently as she brought the words alive. Many thought it was a new type of book signing. We sold eighty-six books that night. I guess it *was* a new type of book signing. We continued this type of innovative approach to book signings and our overall marketing strategy. It worked like a charm.

Worksheet 6:
Marketing Your Book

Your Marketing Plan:

1. Determine your marketing strategy. This will help you and others know exactly what you want to do. Summarize that here.

_____

_____

_____

2. To whom are you marketing? *(You should have decided this in Step one.)* Remind yourself.

_____

_____

_____

_____

3. Where are you going to market? Speak? Write some sources of potential book signings/interviews. Don't stick to traditional outlets.

_____

_____

_____

_____

4. Brainstorm around any gimmicks or unusual marketing ideas. Write your ideas here for tools that might generate publicity, es.postcards, pens,etc.

_____

_____

_____

5. Determine the goals of your marketing plan. For a goal to be successful, it must be measurable and specific. An example of a book related marketing goal might be, "I want to send out fifty press kits and from those generate five book signings over a three month period." Write your goals here. Include one long and one short-term goal.

    _____

    _____

    _____

6. Decide on the action steps do you need to take to reach your goals. Write those here.

    _____

    _____

    _____

7. Design the book signing script you are going to use to secure book signings here. Remember to include your name, your book title, and the date the book will be available. Summarize your book in fifty worse or less. Use this to practice answering the question, "What is your book about?"

    _____

    _____

    _____

    _____

    _____

    _____

    _____

Selected Reading

Kremer, John. *1001 Ways to Market Your Book*. Open Horizons, 2001 (6th ed).

Levinson, Jay. *The Guerilla Marketing Handbook*. Boston: Houghton-Mifflin, 1994.

Rosen, Emanual. *The Anatomy of A Buzz: How to Create Word-Of Mouth-Marketing*. New York: Doubleday, 2000.

Ross, M., Ross., T. *Jump Start Your Book Sales: A Money Making Guide for Authors, Independent Publishers & Small Presses.* Communication Creativity, 1999.

Cole, David. *Complete Guide to Book Marketing*. Allworth Press, 1999.

Blanco, Jodee. *Complete Guide to Book Publicity*. Allworth Press, 2000.

Step 7.

Getting On
The Shelves:
Selling Your Book

Step 7. Getting on the Shelves:
Selling Your Book

C ontrary to popular opinion, this step is one of the easiest of them all, especially if you've followed the previous six steps: you have conjured the muse, built a business, fine-tuned your words, created a masterpiece, printed your book, and promoted yourself. Getting on the shelf should be a piece of cake. Bookstores and libraries are in the business of books, so they need you as much as you need them. They have the brick and mortar (or the online business), and you have the content. It's time to build that ramp and ride your bike sky-high.

Bookstores

Traditionally, bookstores are the primary and premier outlet for selling your masterpiece. I am sure you have seen the many types stores, from small independents such as Vertigo and Karibu Book in Washington, DC, to specialty shops such as Mitchie's and Bookpeople in Austin, TX, to the behemoth chain stores such as Borders and Barnes & Noble. Getting your books on the shelves requires determination, savvy and patience on your part. Remember, they are in business to sell books, so you have to convince them that your book will sell.

As a first step, send your press kit and sample book to the store manager or owner and follow up with a phone call of the most professional manner. More than likely, if you present yourself as a learned book publisher/author, they will agree to stock at least a few copies of your book.

Dealing with the chains is a little more difficult. They have regional and national book buyers who determine what each store will carry, and they tend to spend a majority of their time sifting through the thousands of books that the major publishers release each year. However, with the success of such smaller house-published titles like *Chicken Soup For The Soul*, and *Conversations with God*, these same buyers pay a little more attention to the lesser-known authors and titles. Each of the chains has a small press, or extended title program for writers just like us. Follow their submission procedures and cross your fingers. The Internet is a great tool to use in finding contact information for bookstores around the world. A great way to meet booksellers, small and large, is to visit BEA. This is an extended weekend of seminars, exhibits, conferences, networking and festive celebrations for booksellers, writers, publishers, and industry professionals worldwide. Despite the advent of the Internet and the electronic information age, the best way to get your book on the brick and mortar shelves is to meet the booksellers face to face, or at least phone to phone. Make it personal. I recall reading how a first-time author sent personal letters to over 3000 booksellers across the country, introducing herself and her book. It was expensive, but she wanted to get her name recognized and her books in the stores. The response was phenomenal and today Terry McMillan is a household name and a pretty successful author.

At first, bookstores did not want to carry the *The Book*. Even though we had developed this brilliant marketing campaign, they claimed it was too huge of a risk to stock an unknown author. So we offered to allow them to carry the book on consignment. This is a last resort for the new publisher, as it means that the bookstore will only pay you for what they sell. There is no guarantee that you will make any money through consignment, since the bookseller really has no reason to push the book. It usually just sits there on the shelf. After two months of our marketing efforts, finally the bookstores started carrying and even ordering more books. After three months, the book had sold over 5000 copies and the phones were constantly ringing *off the hook*. Not only bookstores, but libraries and distributors, even agents and editors were calling. Everyone wanted a piece of this book that interested no one in the previous year. The publishers were even calling to see if we were interested in selling the rights.

In less than six months, *That Guy* got his wish, on his own terms, when he sold *The Book* to a major New York publisher (for a hefty five figures, I might add). There were obstacles, but we all maintained clarity of purpose, motivation and direction. *That Guy* is now a best-selling author, with three books in print, and a growing fan club. I also hear that he was able to quit his job and write for a living.

Libraries

If only 10 percent of the libraries in the country order just one copy of your book, you could print an additional 2000 books. Imagine that. In the U.S. librarians not libraries make a majority of book purchases. Attending the Annual American Library Association Conference or the regional, state and local meetings of librarians is a great way to meet librarians, and acquisitions directors from libraries nationwide. Often times, you will be able to contact a country or city library main office and successfully place your books in all the local libraries with just one call. For instance, the main office of the Enoch Pratt Free Library in Baltimore, may purchase sixteen copies of your book, and distribute a copy to each of its branches. This will save you time, long distance charges, and postage. Remember that librarians have an obligation to diversify their holdings and to meet the specific needs of their patrons.

Wholesalers, Jobbers and Distributors

Many novice publishers think of wholesalers and distributors as the same, but there is a major difference between the two. Both stock books in warehouses which they make available to their customers (bookstores, libraries, grocery stores, etc.). Wholesalers and jobbers (library wholesalers), do not promote your work, but rather provide book procurement services to the library and bookstore markets. The largest of the wholesaler/jobbers is Baker & Taylor, with an inventory of some 15 million books.

Distributors such as Bookazine and National Book Network not only warehouse your title(s), but they actively sell and promote your titles. Each has a staff of telemarketers and sales representatives that interact, either by phone or visit, and pitches several titles to the buyers. Somewhere in the middle of the wholesaler/distributor are the large companies such as Ingram, that provide all of these services and many more, in an ala carte cost fashion. Securing a wholesaler is just a matter of process and follow-through, whereas finding a distributor who is willing to sell your title to bookstores requires a track record and proof that your title will indeed make money.

Wholesalers and distributors can prove invaluable, as you only have to deal with one or two accounts payable departments when you are trying to get payment on a past-due invoice. For the first time out, inevitably you will have to deal with 2000 bookstores and libraries individually, but it will provide you with a wealth of knowledge and experience from which to draw when you decide to write your self-publishing tome.

To be or not to be Online

We all know the Internet is supposed to be the great distribution equalizer. The idea of cutting out the aforementioned brick and mortar middleman is exciting and can be increasingly profitable. Selling your titles over the Internet allows you to have a 24-hour one-stop shopping center for your book and its ancillary products. Here are a few online opportunities for you to explore and exploit:

- Amazon.com has a program for self-publishers and independent presses. It's called Amazon Advantage, and allows you to easily sell your books on their site (and receive monthly checks). Other e-commerce sites (sites that allow for credit cards or e-check purchasing of products and services) such as barnesandnoble.com, borders.com, and booksamillion.com also provide you with the opportunity to sell your books online. Visit their sites to determine the specific submission procedures.

- Designing and developing your own e-commerce website cuts out the middleman even more. You can have the site linked directly to your business checking account.
- There are sites like rightsworld.com that enable you to sell different rights (film, foreign, audio) to your title(s) to other companies.

Other Outlets

Book sales are book sales, regardless of their origin. Seek out the following non-traditional outlets in your community:

- Church Bazaars
- Outdoor Festivals
- Book Fairs
- Family Reunions
- Thematic-related film and theatre premiers
- PTA's (no shame, no shame have I)
- Professional meetings of relevant organizations
- Beauty Salons

Having your book in more than one outlet can increase your name recognition, open up different markets for you, and put more money in your pockets.

Sales Terms and Discounts

All of the outlets you sell to will ask for your terms. Prepare a one pager which lists this information, including contact info, return policy (do you accept returned books, and if so, do you issue refund or credit?), pricing, and discount schedule. The following are the price discounts offered to the outlets we've discussed in this chapter.

- Bookstores receive a 40 percent (plus or minus a few points) discount on your book. If the book is ten dollars, they pay six. Typically, they request a *Net 30* Payment Term, which means they can pay you thirty days after receipt of the order. This is your call. If it's someone you know, or you are really trying to get your book in a particular store, you may have to allow *Net 30*. If your book is the best thing since the *Yellow Pages*, you will certainly have more leverage to accept only pre-payment.
- Distributors, wholesalers and jobbers receive a 55-60 percent discount on your book. Distributors are accustomed to receiving a *Net 90*-payment term.
- Online booksellers receive anywhere from 40-60 percent depending on the terms of their agreements. Terms range from pre-payment to *Net 90*.
- Libraries that order single copies of your book tend to get a 20-40 percent discount. Libraries normally pay *Net 30*, and they almost always pay on time.

Fulfillment

Receiving orders will give you a head rush. Fulfilling them will give you a headache. When I started in this business, I was fortunate enough to have a bestseller on my list. I spent most days filling orders, with very little time for administration and other operational duties. This was a blessing in disguise, at it allowed me to systemize my order response system. I allotted certain days of the week to ship UPS (still the best shipping service) and USPS (United States Postal

Service). I chose a computer program that made invoicing simple and multi-functional (Quickbooks). For bookstores that were in a two-hour radius, I devoted one day a week to deliveries (in my car). I suggest that you come up with a similar system that works for you, as it is important for the life of your business to receive orders, but it is double important to fulfill them in a timely manner.

Selling your book is a tedious process of submission, follow-up, confirmation, shipping, invoicing and collecting. Know this process intimately, and continue to bridge your creativity with the functions we've discussed. Follow up daily. This will ensure placement of your product in as many outlets possible.

You've come a long way, and receiving payment for book sales is just one of the many rewards of book publishing. Don't be discouraged when customers don't pay on time, as it will happen. The goal is to find your rhythm, and it will come, as surely as the ride you've taken on this journey.

I would love to tell you that it's over or you're finished. In fact, you've only just started. We know how to ride the bike, pop a wheelie, and maybe even stand on the handlebars. Now is the time to put on our helmet, pack a lunch, oil the chain, and just ride, like a ten year-old boy in the spring. Spread your wings and let your masterpiece ride the steps to publishing success.

Worksheet 7:
Selling Your Book

1. Make a list of the independent and chain bookstores in your area. Find out who buys books at each store. It may or not be the same person who arranges signings.

_____

_____

_____

_____

2. Make of list of non-traditional outlets where you can promote your book _(e.g. beauty salons, churches, etc.)._

_____

_____

_____

_____

3. Make of list of potential wholesalers and distributors. Find out their current information. Write that here.

_____

_____

_____

_____

4. Decide what your terms are going to be for bookstores, libraries and wholesalers. Write that information here. Don't forget to think about your return policy and policy for shipping.

_____

_____

_____

Selected Reading

Logan, Dan and Sandra S. Nichols (Illustrator). *Marketing and Selling Your Books on the Internet*, 2000.

Pitner, Suzanne F. *Selling Old Books the New Dot Com Way: Your Guide to Starting and Running an Internet Bookselling Business.* IUniverse.com, 2000.

Poynter, Dan *Book Fulfillment: Order Entry, Picking, Packing and Shipping.* California: Para Publishing, 1997.

Woodham, Roger. *Book Distribution (Publisher's Guide Series).* Chapman & Hall, 1991.

Mandino, Og. *The Greatest Salesman in The World.* New York: Bantam Books, 1983.

Rolnicki, Kenneth. *Managing Channels of Distribution.* Amacom, 1997.

Appendices

Appendix A:

Who Said Poetry Doesn't Sell?
Publishing and Promoting Your Poems

Contemporary publishers don't publish poetry en masse (like fiction, spiritual, how-to, and everything else) because they don't believe that poetry books sell. That's partly true. Most readers just don't walk into a bookstore and ask for the poetry section. (They should!) At the same time, if a reader happens upon a poetry reading at a Starbucks or jazz club, they are both attentive and intrigued. I believe that major publishers shy away from verse because they don't know "The Secret": *poets sell books*. (Some do anyway.)

Eventually poetry will sell itself, as it has in the past, but right now, published poets need to understand the correlation between performance and profit. In 1994, I produced a poetry showcase featuring different local poets. Some were trained academic poets, while others were street poets. Since there was no admission cost to the event, I had to devise a plan to make some money to pay the starving artists. My bright idea was to publish a compilation of poems from the participants in the showcase. We printed one hundred copies at the local Kinko's, and had them prominently displayed at the showcase, which was well attended by three hundred people. Within thirty minutes following the end of the show, all the books were sold, and a dozen or so patrons attempted to order copies. *The Secret.*

In 1995, I was in the midst of a twenty-city book tour with a poet whom I'd published. We were visiting a church in Los Angeles, and as it turned out, the pastor knew my poet. After the service, she was asked to read a poem (just one), which she did. Fortunately, I had several (six to be exact) cases of books in my rental trunk. Within thirty minutes following the church service, over 150 books had been sold at an informal book signing for my poet. The Secret.

I could go on and on about the secret, but it should be pretty clear. When people think of poetry, they might think of the Robert Frost they were forced to read in grade school, or some other painful remembrance. However, when people hear poetry they can become excited, inspired and interested in reading more from the poet. It is this combination of poetry and what we will call "spoken word," that leads to increased profits from the sales of poetry books. Of course, it is the responsibility of individual poets to learn, harness and promote the performance aspect of their art.

In my travels, I am often asked the question, "What do you recommend to poets looking to get published?" Here is my top seven list: Write, Rewrite, Write, and Rewrite your poems (Practice makes . . .)

1. Submit your work to journals, literary magazines and online publications (Gets your name out there, while giving you more literary credibility).
2. Read, Reread, Read, and Reread poetry books, history books, and any book you can get your hands on. (Broaden your knowledge, so you will have something to write about besides you.)
3. Read and/or perform your poems at open mic's, and slams. (This will help you develop and sustain your

performance technique.) Keep in mind, performance can mean reading your poems with a theatrical flair, or it could mean memorizing your poems and acting them out.

4. When you are ready to publish, choose the best 100 of your poems. Throw fifty of them away, and choose the best forty of the remaining ones. Rewrite those, and choose the best thirty. Thirty poems are usually good for a first poetry book or chapbook (smaller saddle-stitched book). This may seem harsh, but it's important that after you wow the audiences at your readings, they take the book home and still enjoy.

5. Self-publish your first poetry book, or work with a collective of writers. (This will give you more control, and you know how we poets like control.)

6. Lastly, read, perform and promote as much as possible. Everything you've done until now is useless unless you take your poetry from the page to the stage.

Appendix B:
Production Schedule

The Book
Author: (That Guy)
Designer: (Artsy Fartsy)
Editor: (Make it Better)
Copyeditor/Proofreader: (Red Penned Maniac)

	Proposed	Actual
Complete Final Draft:	11/17	
Draft to Editor:	11/20	
Design Template Complete:	12/15	
Edited Draft to Author:	1/20	
Rewrite Complete:	2/20	
Draft 2 to Editor:	2/21	
Rewrite Complete:	3/10	
Copy to Type/Design:	3/11	
Send Specs to Printers:	3/15	
A Pages to Copyediting:	4/7	
A Pages to Author:	4/14	
A Pages to Type/Design:	4/17	
B Pages to Copyediting:	4/25	
B Pages to Type/Design:	5/1	
Final Pages to Copyediting:	5/5	
Final Pages to Type/Design:	5/7	
Final Pages to "Clean Eyes":	5/12	
Final Pages to Author;	5/15	
Final 2 Pages to Type/Design:	5/18	
To Printer:	5/19	

	Proposed	Actual
Proof in:	6/1	
Proof out:	6/3	
Off press:	6/25	
Deliver to Storage:	6/27	
Publication Date:	8/1	

Marketing is not considered a production function, it has its own schedule with heavy overlap. Also, depending on your workflow, you may need to shorten or lengthen the time increments of your schedule.

Appendix C:
Bidding Specifications Sheet

To: Customer Service Contact/Printing Company
From: Kwame Alexander, Random Mouse
Date: March 13
Project: The Book by That Guy

****

Quote: Please Fax Quote to Kwame Alexander at
             512-555-5555 by March 20
Pages: 288 plus cover
Quantity: 3000
Size: 6" x 9"
Stock: Text: 55# Natural
             Cover: 10 pt C1S
Binding: Perfect Bound
Ink: Text: 1/1
             Cover: 4/0
Art: Text: Zip Disk provided in Quark 4.0 for the Mac
             Cover: Zip Disk provided in Quark 4.0 for the Mac
Proof: Blueline and Matchprint
             (Please advise when we can expect)
Schedule: Project to Printer May 19; Off-press on June 25.
Delivery: 1. 10 Samples to attn: Kwame Alexander,
                2222 ABC Street, Apt 1111, Austin, TX
             2. Balance to Public Storage, Lot 17, 1111
                ABC Boulevard, Austin, TX
Queries: Kwame Alexander at 512-555-5555 or
             kwame_alexander@RandomMouse.com

Appendix D:
Book Signing Work Plan

Three to Four Months
Contact bookstores to arrange signings/readings.
Produce a detailed book signing schedule (include in all
    promotional packages)

Four to Six Weeks
Send confirmation to bookstore by mail or fax including
    press materials, responsibilities, special requirements
    (e.g. microphone), number of books ordered.
Accommodations and transportation arranged
Send press kits and contact local media outlets for guest
    appearances and coverage

2 Weeks
Verification of promotional activities (radio, tv, etc.)
Author receives itinerary from bookstore and local
    publicity contacts
Final shipping to bookstore
Plan and practice for reading

1 Week
Reconfirm all travel accommodations, directions, meals,
    prep time, etc.

1-2 day
Travel

Event Day

Set up

Walk through

Sign books until your fingers ache!

Appendix E:
Basic Marketing Timeline

Four to Six Months
Start Telling Family and Friends about your book
Send press kits and review copies to periodicals, magazines
and interested parties

Three Months
Design and develop a website
Search online for places to list your book
Begin setting up signings and appearances
Follow-up with possible reviews and feature articles

One to Two Months
Send press kit to bookstores
Firm up the book signing schedule
Send out postcards and emails to friends, associates, and
    other mailing lists

On-going
Refine and add to your press kit as needed. Try to send a
    new press release about your book at least every
    3 months.

Appendix F:
Selected Vendors

Publishing Consultants

Kwame Alexander
Woodbridge, VA
blackwordsinc@cs.com

Nina Foxx
Austin, TX
neenah@austin.rr.com

Editors

EEI
Washington, DC
Contact: Steven Colgan
http://www.eeicommunications.com

Barbara Williams Lewis, Ph.D.
The Red Pen
Austin, TX
bleweis@austin.cc.tx.us

Jennifer Steptoe Rhodes
Woodbridge, VA
jmariar@aol.com

Pentouch Literary
Dallas, TX
Contact: Moni Blache
http://www.pentouch.com

Book Designers/Desktop Publishers

Kim Greyer Graphic Design
Austin, TX
512/288-5677
Kgreyer@aol.com

Kyle Design Group
Bethesda, MD
Contact: Joseph Jones
http://www.kyledesigngroup.com

Artists/Illustrators

John Ashford
Brooklyn, NY
John Ashford1@hotmail.com

The Creative Group
Washington, DC
Contact: Janet Tibbs
http://www.creativegroup.com

Adjoa Burrows
Alexandria, VA
Adjoa4art@aol.com

Printers

Thomson Shore Book Manufacturers
Ann Arbor, MI
Contact: Christine Blanke
http://www.thomson-shore.com

Whitehall Book Printing
Coral Gables, FL
Contact: Roxanne Shenker
http://www.whitehallprinting.com

KCR Docutech Printing
Washington, DC
Contact: Elvis Lewis
http://www.kcrdpi.com

Marketing Firms

Phenix & Phenix
Austin, TX
http://www.Bookpros.com

Manisy Willows Marketing & Distribution Services
Austin, TX
Contact: Beryl Horton
www.ManisyWillows.com
manisywillowsbooks@austin.rr.com

Tri-Com
Rockford, IL
Contact: Peggy Hicks
http://www.tricomweb.com/

Distributors

Biblio/NBN
Lanhan, MD
Contact: Dina Fullerton
http://www.bibliodistribution.com

Small Press Distribution
Berkeley, CA
Contact: Heather Peeler
http://www.spdbooks.org

Culture Plus Wholesalers
New York, NY
Contact: Larry

Website Designers/Developers

Jamila White
Washington, DC
http://www.Jamilawhite.com

The Creative Group
Washington, DC
Contact: Allison Parker
http://www.creativegroup.com

Kim Greyer Graphic Design
Austin, TX
Kgreyer@aol.com

The authors have successfully worked with, or know professionals who have worked with the above-listed vendors.

Appendix G:
Websites of Interest

http://ajr.newslink.org - Listings of Media outlets by City

http://artworld.ddwi.com - Art, Design Resources

http://www.bookmarket.com/ - Book Publishing/
Marketing Resources

http://www.btol.com/corporate - Baker & Taylor Books

http://www.eReleases.com/ - e-Marketing Resource

http://www.literarymarketplace.com - Book Industry
Resources

http://www.blackwordsonline.com - Multi-cultural literary
ezine and e-commerce site

http://www.m-w.com/ - Merriam-Webster Online Dictionary
and Thesaurus

http://www.netlibrary.com - e-book resources

http://www.netread.com/ - Event, Signings Listing

http://nt9.nyic.com/literaryagent/sch-page.html -
Agent Listing

http://www.pma-online.org/ - Publishers Marketing
Association

http://www.spannet.org - Small Publishers Resources and
Organizations

http://www.u-publish.com - e-book information &
publishing pointers

http://www.write-brain.com/ - Resource for Creative
Writers

http://writerexchange.about.com/library/weekly/
aa020300a.htm - Literary Agent Resource and Information

Glossary

Acquisition Editors- The person at a publishing company in charge of reviewing and rating incoming manuscripts for possible publication and then supervise the publication process.

Advance- A sum paid to the author in anticipation of royalty earnings.

American Booksellers Association (ABA)- American Booksellers Association is a not-for-profit trade organization devoted to meeting the needs of its core members – independently owned bookstores with store front locations – through advocacy, education, research, and information dissemination

Appendix- Supplementary materials printed at the end of the general text.

Audience- The group most likely to be interested in the subject matter of the book.

Back Matter- The section after the body of the text and may include the endnotes, index, bibliography, author biography, etc.

Bar Code- A system of stripes and bars printed on the back cover of a book. Used universally in the book industry for automated ordering and inventory systems.

Binding- The process if affixing pages together in a single bound book.

Blueline- The proof sheet(s) of a books revealed in bluish ink that shows exactly how the pages or cover of a book will look when it is printed.

Blurb- Abbreviated, positive review of the book or the author often appearing on the back cover or in front matter.

Book- A bound publication of 49 or more pages that is not a magazine or periodical.

BookExpo America (BEA)- formerly known as the American Booksellers Association Convention & Trade Exhibit, is an education forum, a center of rights activity and the meeting place for the entire publishing industry.

Books in Print- A database managed by R. R. Bowker of books in or about to print based on the ISBN numbers issued by them to the publishers.

Camera-ready- Final artwork, including typesetting and graphics ready for reproduction in the final book production process.

CIP- Cataloging in Publication. The bibliographic information supplied by the Library of Congress and printed on the copyright page

Clip Art- Generic graphics that can be "clipped out" and used for illustrations. Available on the Internet and software programs for not charge.

Content Edit- An edit of a book that checks the flow of the text, its organization, continuity and content.

Copy Edit- An edit that checks for grammar, spelling, punctuation and other "typos."

Copyright- Legal protection given to intellectual rights such written and published works in a variety of forms such as books, audio and software.

Cover Art- the design of the book jacket,

Design- Artistic process placing images and/or words into camera ready copy.

Desktop Publishing- Book design, layout, and production completed on a personal computer by specific software.

Distributor- A company that buys books from a publisher or other distributors and resells them to retail accounts.

E-book- Electronic Book- A book published in electronic form that can be downloaded to computers or handheld devices.

Editing- Changing or correcting the contents of a book in order to improve the final results or to fit a format.

EIN- Employer Identification Number. Issued by the Federal Government to business for tax purposes. A Social Security Number may be used as an EIN in some businesses.

Epilogue- Additional text at the end of the book, that provides readers with additional information on the subject.

Final draft- The final proof after all other proofing and editing steps have been completed.

Focus Group- A small cross section of people brought together to provide feedback on marketing ideas and products.

Font- The typeset used in page design.

Foreign Rights- Rights granted or sold that allows books to be printed and sold in other countries.

Four Color Process- Using the major colors magenta, cyan, yellow and black to produce pictures in a range of colors.

Freelance - An independent contractor hired to work on a book, design or marketing plan.

Front Matter- The series of pages that appear before the body of text.

Galley- The pre-publication copies sent to the author for final proofreading or to reviewers for pre-publication reviews.

Genre- A specific category of literature, marked by a distinctive style form or content.

Graphics- The non-type parts of a book such as drawings, illustrations, photographs, charts, etc. that are used to enhance the content of a book.

Hard Copy- A print out of the manuscript.

Imprint- The name of the publishing company on the title page.

ISBN- International Standard Book Number- An identification number code uniquely assigned to every book and obtained from the R. R. Bowker company.

Jobber- A type of distributor who provides books to that works on a smaller scale than wholesalers and provides mass market titles to airports, grocery stores, drug stores, etc.

Library of Congress- The national library of the United States located in Washington D.C.

List Price- The sales price printed on your book or the retail sales price.

Logo- Identification mark used by an individual, business or organization as a representation symbol.

Manuscript- The book in typewritten or word processing form.

Marketing Plan- A book selling plan that includes a budget, synopsis of book, target audience, distribution, promotion, timeline and how you will create demand.

Mass Market- A small format paperback edition usually sold in airports, grocery stores and drug stores.

Media Kit- See Media Kit.

Mid-list- a title or author that does not become a bestseller

Out of Print- a title no longer maintained in the publisher's catalogue or inventory

Preface- The introductory portion of the book that usually explains why the book was written, what it is about or how to use it.

Press Kit- Provides reporters, reviewers, bookstore managers and others information on the book. It includes a press release, author biography, book cover, testimonials, etc.

Proofreader- Checks the manuscript to make certain that the copy is correct and verified before final printing.

Publication Date- The date set, usually after actual printing of the book, that is announced to let the target audience know when the book will be available.

Publicity- A marketing technique using free advertising outlets such as press releases.

Publisher- The person or company responsible for the entire process of producing books. This includes overseeing the writing, editing, design, production, printing and marketing of the book.

Review- A critical evaluation of a book.

Review Copy- A free copy given away to be reviewed.

Royalties- percentage of the sales price earned by the author on sold copies. These are generally charged against the advance until it is earned out.

Spine- The binding on the side of a book.

Subsidiary Rights- Additional rights, such as foreign, audio, serial to publish a book in a different form.

The American Library Association provides leadership for the development, promotion, and improvement of library and information services and the profession of librarians.

Title- Name of a book.

Trim- The final dimension of a book after the printer or bindery has cut it to size.

Typesetting- A term that originally referred to the setting of lead type for printing presses or phototypesetting. With advancing technology nearly all "typesetting" is now done on the computer.

Vanity Press- A waning term as the name implies a "Vanity Press" is a publisher that produces books with the author paying all costs and maintaining all ownership. Vanity Presses most commonly do not allow author input other than paper color and binding style.

Website - A location on the Internet accessible by inputting a unique address that provides information on a subject, person or organization..

Wholesaler- A central order location that allows bookstores and libraries to order multiple titles from multiple publishers.

Word of Mouth- Advertising generated by satisfied or interested readers who tell others about the book.

Index

A

B

C

E

F

G

Q

R

S

About The Author

E.C. Kwame Alexander is a publishing consultant and the founder of a well known independent publishing house based in the Washington, D.C. Area. He has also written two screenplays and five stageplays and is the author/editor of four books. Through his publishing and consulting, he has led many authors to success. He lives in Alexandria, Virginia.

Nina Foxx' innovative marketing ideas has helped her book, *Dippin' My Spoon*, appear on numerous best seller lists.

Wanna Ride Some More?

Now that you've hopped on the bike to publishing success, let a trained professional guide you along the detailed path to a rewarding literary future.

Kwame Alexander
PO Box 21
Alexandria, VA 22313
Blackwordsinc@cs.com
703-494-3363 (phone and fax)

Manisy Willows Books
Nina Foxx
701 Capital of Texas Hwy., Bldg. C
P. O. Box 1202
Austin, TX 78746
ManisyWillowsBooks@austin.rr.com
512/347-9995 Voice
512/347-9996 Fax

Coming Soon:

Do The Write Thing Workbook *(w/Video)*, and Say The Write Thing: 7 Steps to Presentation Success.